W9-CAL-986

Only one power in all this universe can rescue us from what we are and what we've done—the massive grace of God in Jesus. But how small are our thoughts of His grace! Eric Mason expands our minds with his daring new book, all "to the praise of His glorious grace."

Ray Ortlund, Pastor, Immanuel Church
in Nashville, Tennessee, and author of *The Gospel:
How the Church Portrays the Beauty of Christ*

Eric Mason is truly one of the great young voices of this generation. *Beat God to the Punch* is a prescription for every believer. Eric speaks about grace in a high definition format that draws your heart, your head, and your hands into living it out thoroughly. I was incredibly enriched by his treatment of grace in both a classic and contemporary sense. Reading this book will enrich and enlarge your view of this most important part of the Christian life. I challenge you to read it, share it, and meditate upon the truths of God's grace packaged in this work.

Bryan Carter, Senior Pastor,
Concord Church in Dallas, Texas

Beat God to the Punch is a theologically robust inspiring challenge for all to submit to the Lordship of Jesus Christ. My friend Eric Mason reminds us that God's wrath has been satisfied on the cross through the finished work of Jesus Christ, and it is this incomprehensible grace that is to inspire our joyful submission, not guilt. I am hopeful that much fruit will come from this great book!

Bryan Loritts, Lead Pastor, Fellowship Memphis,
and author of *Right Color, Wrong Culture*

I often encounter sermons and books about grace that leave me wondering where costly discipleship fits in. Other times, I hear the call to discipleship, but I'm left gasping for grace. Eric Mason gives us robust discipleship in the context of overwhelming grace. For fusing these two themes into one coherent message, *Beat God to the Punch* commands attention.

Hunter Beaumont, Pastor, Fellowship Denver

Eric Mason leads us to a deeper understanding of God's grace and how it embodies who God is. But what I like best are the stories he shares of how his experiences as an inner-city church planter and pastor have caused him to depend on grace in a new way and have challenged him to extend it to others. Grace brings hope to people who are broken and have no other way out. This book will cause you to view grace in a new way and to see yourself and others through God's "grace potential."

Kevin Ezell, President, North American Mission Board

BEAT GOD TO THE PUNCH

BECAUSE JESUS DEMANDS YOUR LIFE

ERIC MASON

FOREWORD BY PAUL DAVID TRIPP

PUBLISHING GROUP

NASHVILLE, TENNESSEE

To my wife Yvette,

*God's grace has been a staple of our journey with Him
and with one another.*

*To experience all of the illnesses and losses you have,
and to be free of all bitterness and resentfulness is a joy to watch.*

*I dedicate this book to you, enjoying every season of your life with the
strength of the good Lord. Love you, babe, and I'm thankful to be
encountering the grace of God through life with you.*

ACKNOWLEDGMENTS

Thanks to the Lord Jesus Christ for doing exceedingly abundantly above all that I have asked or thought. The fact that I am writing (and now enjoying it) is a miracle from heaven. Lord, only You could stir my affections for these things.

I would like to thank the staff at B&H for their commitment to the gospel and sound biblical output. I cannot thank the Lord enough for you guys. Big shout-out to Devin Maddox for his encouragement and support through this process.

Epiphany Fellowship, I'm thankful daily that you are the local church I get to serve. It is an honor. I'm thankful for your encouragement to remain committed to writing. Your encouragement goes a long way with my heart, and I am eternally grateful.

Thriving team: thank for your encouragement and service as well. You guys are the best.

CONTENTS

FOREWORD

The location: Camden, New Jersey

The scene: Epiphany Church Camden

The event: Good Friday service

The atmosphere: Celebration of the grace of the cross of Jesus

Luella and I went to the service not really knowing what to expect. We left blown away with what we had experienced and with hearts filled with gratitude for God's amazing grace. We listened that night to a company of young preachers winsomely expound and practically apply the words of Christ on the cross. We really were blown away by the street-level theology and the transformative practicality of what we heard that evening. I love hearing good preaching. I love having my heart rattled. I love looking at life through the lens of the cross of Jesus. At the end of the service I felt like a man who had just done a whole lot of grazing at a very good buffet. My heart and my brain were full, but I was sad when the service ended.

All the young, budding theologians who spoke that evening were mentored/discipled by Eric Mason or by someone who had been mentored/discipled by Eric Mason. As I read the manuscript of this book, it hit me that Eric had taught these young men to do exactly what this book is about. You could hear it in their words, and you could feel it in their passion. It was no accident that these men spoke with such confident clarity. They had been taught to "beat God to the punch."

Now, maybe you're thinking, *Paul, what in the world are you talking about? We can't ever beat God to the punch. He is in control. He is sovereign. He always is the one who initiates our relationship with Him. Isn't the Bible the origin-to-destiny story of how God in grace has beaten us to the punch? There is something about this phrase that just doesn't seem right.*

Well, it is true. Every moment of thought, desire, choice, and decision that moves us toward God is initiated by His rescuing, forgiving, transforming, and delivering grace. Without the move of His grace, we would remain in our sin—spiritually dead men walking. There is a way in which it is perverse for us to take any credit whatsoever for the spiritual awakening, submission, and growth in our lives. The apostle Paul says that if it is all God's gift then there is simply no room at all for personal boasting. We must all remember the desperate and hopeless condition we were all in before glorious, powerful grace entered our door.

But with the phrase "beat God to the punch" Mason is onto something—something important, something that could change your life. Now, it's not that the Christian life is up to you. There are some that teach this. God by grace brings you in and by grace takes you out, and in between it's up to you. If in between my spiritual life is left to my fickle and wandering heart, I'm cooked. What a hopeless view of what goes on between the "already" and the "not yet." No, what Mason is proposing by his provocative phrase is that the grace-filled, grace-dependent, grace-hopeful life is not a passive life. It's not sitting around waiting for grace to do its work. It's not "letting go and letting God." It's not taking a vacation on Jesus.

Yes, your hope is in God's grace and God's grace alone. You never, ever rely on your performance, but the grace-filled, grace-dependent life is an active right. It takes grace to reach out for grace, but that's exactly what God calls you to do. The grace-dependent life is a life of *joyfully active rest*. God's grace doesn't relieve you of activity; it ignites God-honoring, joyful activity. It celebrates the eternal liberty of a brand new way of living.

In grace God calls you to activity. He says,

"Seek Me."

"Love Me."

"Trust Me."

"Follow Me."

"Serve Me."

"Worship Me."

"Beating God to the punch" is about reaching out for what you could have never earned, achieved, or deserved. It is affirming your desperate need for what only grace can provide. It is celebrating the shocking sacrifice of the Messiah for your sins. It is embracing the nowism of the grace of Jesus. It's celebrating your freedom from your slavery to sin and your welcome to slavery to Christ. Obedience is your moral obligation, but it is never, ever your means of achieving or maintaining relationship with God. You reach out knowing that in the moments when you don't reach out, God will still not turn His back on you. But you don't sit around waiting. You run after the grace that has eternally taken hold of and rescued you from you. Mason would say that you "beat God to the punch." And I'm glad for the reminder. Read and you will be too.

Paul David Tripp
5/2/14

INTRODUCTION

Hearing this title will raise many eyebrows—especially if one knows anything about the character and nature of the living God. This title is meant to draw the reader into the complexities (and simplicity) of a grace-filled life. God is the all-knowing Sovereign Lord. He is God all by Himself and doesn't need anybody else. How can someone *beat God to the punch*?

One day, God's wrath and glory is going to be revealed to everyone, and all will have to acknowledge the Lordship of the Mighty One, Jesus Christ. Philippians 2:9–11 makes it clear:

> For this reason God highly exalted Him and gave Him the name that is above every name, so that at the name of Jesus every knee will bow—of those who are in heaven and on earth and under the earth—and every tongue should confess that Jesus Christ is Lord, to the glory of God the Father.

This is a reality, that all will bow to Jesus. By implication, we have the option to bow by choice, or to bow by force. This reality extends to our whole life. Willfully bowing to Jesus now—rather than later—is the option we have in our everyday life. The preaching of the gospel is the invitation—a free offer, an urgent call—to bow now, by choice.

In our willingness to bow, we find a grace-filled existence in our walk with the Lord Jesus Christ. Beating God to the punch involves willingly bending one's life to Jesus now, and forever. Practice begins by trusting in the finished work of Jesus Christ on the cross and His resurrection from the dead as a substitutionary atonement for your sin. Upon the return of Jesus, all will acknowledge His Lordship. On that day, those who are forced to bow will experience the punch of God's wrath. Those who willingly bow at the appointed time of salvation will be missed by God's wrathful punch because God hit Jesus on their behalf.

How to Seize a Grace-Filled Life

For those who have a relationship with God through Jesus Christ, this is a process by which we fight, through His power, to live a grace-filled life. This grace-filled life is the willingness to continue to progressively set Jesus aside as Lord every day. First Peter 3:15 states, "But honor the Messiah as Lord in your hearts. Always be ready to give a defense to anyone who asks you for a reason for the hope that is in you."

Our hearts are the epicenter of our values, affections, and will. Jesus is to be given the top position in our hearts. As a result, the Lordship of Jesus dominates every aspect of our heart. In fighting for this reality the believer *beats God to the punch,* because we willingly worship and adore Jesus before the universe is forced to bow before His glorious might.

On the other hand, those who are not in a relationship with Jesus will, in unison with those who value the Christ, bow by force. Those who refuse to respond to the glorious gospel will have to one day admit that the One they rejected is the One who deserved their all. Although this bowing will occur among those who reject the gospel, this bow will not merit salvation because the time will be up. Therefore, we will implore you to place all your confidence in the one who is worthy of our life, because He gave His life as a ransom for us. This will cause us to beat God to the punch.

Jesus, in John 1:35–51, graciously invites some young men to experience this grace-filled life. Jesus' interaction with them leads up to a climax where He invites them to willingly participate in the revelation of His Lordship now (in smaller trailers), and later (in the ultimate eschatological movie of His return). Throughout this resource we will refer to this passage as a compass of what it looks like to come in contact with God's grace in the person of Jesus Christ. In addition, it will serve us in Jesus pointing us to joyously experiencing all things being brought to conclusion. We will find ourselves looking in other places in the Word of God for the echoes of God's grace in those places.

Let's be clear: beating God to the punch is never accomplished through our own effort, enlightenment, strength, or power. Only by God's grace is one able to bow. We will explore the recesses of how grace gives the strength to us to bow our lives to the living God. Without grace we are helpless and hopeless in living a life filled with joy and the true happiness that comes from God through Jesus Christ. Interestingly enough, we will find that it isn't through con-trived circumstances, but through the mundane to the magnificent seasons in life where grace works in us to a life lived on our knees walking with and serving the living God.

At times, it will seem as if this book is more about grace than anything else. If the reader walks away with that, the Lord has used this resource to my heart's desire. I want the reader to view this as a tool that motivates them to submit to the Lordship of Jesus Christ by seeing it as a grace from heaven.

Jesus Demands Your Life

Jesus demands your whole life. Not part of it, but the whole. Much has been written on the subject of the Lordship of Jesus Christ. I will not dive into these various arguments on whether to be a Jesus follower and submitting to the Lordship of Jesus Christ should be the content of the presentation that one would hear in order for it to be an authentic communication of the gospel and/or an authentic conversion. As one looks into the content of the Scripture, what is clear is that both the Lordship of Jesus was explained to some prior to salvation and all post conversion. We see Jesus telling unbelieving Pharisees of His Lordship. He states in Matthew 12:8, "For the Son of Man is Lord of the Sabbath." By saying that He is "Lord of the Sabbath," Jesus is communicating that He has equality with God. In doing so, He communicates the extent of His Lordship over them, in this case, specifically as it relates to the Sabbath. They couldn't properly respond to His Lordship because they rejected Him. Belief in Jesus acknowledges Him as an authority in our lives, such that whatever He communicates to us about Himself (whether difficult or palatable), we believe by faith. Though belief that "Jesus is Lord" does not affect His status as Lord, belief does connect us to Him as willing, submissive subjects.

For example, think about a king—essentially, another word for lord. For Americans who are inundated with democracy, it is more difficult to imagine, but there are places in the world where a king rules with absolute power. Regardless of what the subjects of the kingdom think about his leadership, regardless of how they align themselves with his political views, and regardless of how he represents their nation, the king reigns over the entire kingdom. In order to thrive in that kingdom, the people have one of two choices. Either they can recognize the authority of the king, or they can live in rebellion toward the throne.

In the same way, Jesus has established a kingdom that knows no political boundaries. It extends over the entire universe. All, in heaven and on earth, are His subjects. He rules over them regardless of their acknowledgment of His reign. But Jesus doesn't rule like the kings we are accustomed to seeing. His reign is marked by benevolent, generous grace. Who wouldn't want to pledge allegiance to a king like that?

The apostles embraced the Lordship of Jesus over every area of their lives. When Peter and other disciples are faced with responding to Jesus' Lordship as believers, they are faced with a choice between bowing and rebellion. In John's gospel, Jesus makes a culturally and theologically confrontational statement to the crowds and those who are following Him:

> So Jesus said to them, "I assure you: Unless you eat the flesh of the Son of Man and drink His blood, you do not have life in yourselves." . . . From that moment many of His disciples turned back and no longer accompanied Him. (John 6:53, 66)

Subsequently, Jesus' statement was truth that required trust in His character that would allow for Him to bring the clarity necessary for growth. When following, the believer will be faced with hard statements. These hard statements must be processed in relationship with the Lord and giving Him the benefit of the doubt. Some who were "following Him," didn't trust His character enough to sustain their allegiance, and disassociated themselves from Him as the Lord. Those who hung in there with Jesus would later have what was difficult to understand—what the apostle Paul calls the mystery of the gospel in Ephesians—revealed as they continued to trust in Him. Jesus asks a probing question and Peter states by faith,

> Therefore Jesus said to the Twelve, "You don't want to go away too, do you?" Peter's statement is what each stage of our journey with the Lord must be. Peter replied: "Lord, who will we go to? You have the words of eternal life." (John 6:67–68)

Real life, for a disciple, is a journey of wrestling with a pattern of faith and loyalty to who Jesus is. It is a journey often marked by misunderstanding and perplexity. Yet trust and loyalty to a God who doesn't explain everything immediately, nor remove the complexity of following Him, is the means He has chosen to make us more like His Son. In the complexity of pursuing a grace-filled life, we are called to simple (not simplistic) devotion to His glorious Lordship (2 Cor. 11:2–3). Walking with Jesus is recognizing that sometimes He explains immediately (Matt. 12:18–23), sometimes He explains later (John 12:26), or not at all (Acts 1:6–7). Yet we are called to a ferocious commitment to His divine authority. We must refuse to view what He doesn't explain or reveal to us in our time as a credibility issue. We must embrace the beauty of the mystery of the gospel.

The Big Picture

Ultimately this book is about the punch of His wrath, justice, and judgment. As much as we'd like to ignore it, God's wrath can only be quenched under the weight of the cross. Those outside of Jesus don't stand a chance. God's wrath was fully satisfied by Jesus' death (Rom. 5:9), but without the work of Jesus Christ absorbing His wrath, we will experience the consequences of our sin. We must see His Lordship in light of both the law and grace. The law helps us to see His Lordship as righteous and holy. Grace helps us to see His Lordship as inviting us through Jesus to be in relationship to Him. So the question is, will you experience the grace that comes through Jesus Christ to deter that wrath? Or will you be forced to bow? This book is for you.

But this book is also about the life available to those who embrace Jesus as Lord, those who willingly bow the knee. God not only saves us *from* something, He also saves us *for* something. This book is for those who long to thrive in the King's kingdom right now. This book is for you.

So, believer, will you seize the life made available to you in Christ (1 Tim. 6:12), and to the unbeliever, will you be beckoned to seize that life you don't have through what Jesus has done on your behalf (2 Cor. 5:20)?

Let's beat God to the punch.

1

CROSSING PATHS WITH GRACE

> When I saw you the first time,
> I know not what I saw in you. But from
> that moment on, I felt as if everything was really new.
> —Arijit Mandal, *My Love at First Sight*

I have heard many speak of having experienced love at first sight. But I don't know if I have ever experienced it. To be able to love someone without any knowledge of who they are, what they believe, and represent has always seemed a bit of a stretch. Love is not based on our infatuation with a person, but is a choice connected to the knowledge of the good, bad, and ugly of a person. God's love is deeply entrenched in His full knowledge of what we are like.

On the other hand—to return that love toward Him—God must grace us to recognize Him through transformation. We cannot see the glory of God's grace without God changing us to see it. God, the Holy Spirit, does this by aiding us in getting new sight (2 Cor. 3–4; 1 Cor. 12:3). In some sense we do have love at first sight, because our new sight through the gospel helps us to love the One who first loved us. Being dead in our sin, we cannot see God's grace (Eph. 2:1–3). Yet when God opens our eyes with new sight, we can see and respond to the divine image (2 Cor. 3:18).

To be honest, this makes me want to have a praise break for the Ruler of all things. In His unrivaled goodness, He saw fit to give sight to the blind. The greatest sight of the life of the believer is being able to recognize the grace of God.

Grace Walked By

> *Amazing Grace, how sweet the sound, That saved a*
> *wretch like me. I once was lost but now am found, Was blind,*
> *but now I see.* (John Newton, "Amazing Grace")

Grace is a concept that will take us an eternity to come to grips with. It is a massive concept in the Bible. Grace on many occasions has been called "God's unmerited favor." As God's unmerited favor, grace is God choosing to place His affections on us and thereby lavishing us with Himself through the person and work of Jesus. God grants good standing before Him, and He does so without our assistance.

Grace is also defined as all of the goodness of life that is accomplished by God's own doing. No other faith, religion, or belief system has at its foundation the concept of grace. For the Christian, it is both its foundation and all-encompassing tenant.

> One of the distinctive features of the religion of the Bible. No other system of religious thought, past or present, contains an emphasis on divine grace comparable to that of the Bible.

As a general definition, the doctrine of grace pertains to God's activity rather than to his nature. Although God is gracious, this trait of his nature is revealed only in relation to his created works and to his redemptive enterprise. In other words, grace is to be understood in terms of a dynamic expression of the divine personality rather than as a static attribute of God's nature. Grace is the dimension of divine activity that enables God to confront human indifference and rebellion with an inexhaustible capacity to forgive and to bless. God is gracious in action.[1]

Grace is not merely an esoteric theological concept, but it is seen and defined most vehemently in a person.

Jesus is the full embodiment of God's grace. John 1:14 states that Jesus is "full of grace and truth." Being full of grace means that Jesus, in His incarnation, perfectly reflected God's glory in that all of His life and ministry was saturated with grace. Until Jesus came on the scene, grace wasn't a concept that was clear to the world. Although God, in many ways in the Old Testament, displayed His grace to the children of Israel as individuals and as a whole, Jesus fully revealed the commitment of God to man in His incarnation.

For the entirety of this book, we will investigate how Jesus engages us to walk with Him as His disciples under His Lordship through the gospel of grace. The Gospels, whether the Synoptics or John's (as a stand-alone work), act to do one unifying thing and one thing only—to reveal Jesus. Matthew reveals Him mainly as King, Mark as the Suffering Servant, Luke presents the Lord as Son of Man, and crescendos with John revealing Him as God.

The most powerful thing about the Gospels is seeing Jesus reveal Himself to people and their response to His revelation. In

John 1:35–51 we find an encounter with Jesus by some of the future apostles prior to Luke 5 where Jesus reengages them and calls them to mission with Him. After they experience Jesus in John 1, they go back to their normal lives, but Jesus casts an abnormal vision. The vision was compelling enough for them to leave everything to follow Him. Later, Jesus fervently engages in prayer to the Father and calls this motley crew to be His key agents of mission, church planting, and theological pioneering. In our current passage in John, Jesus has His first encounter with the disciples. Jesus meets these guys where they are, but also gives them hope for beyond where they are.

John the Baptist twice expresses the fact that Jesus is the grace of God among men. Twice he states "Behold, the Lamb of God." He is like, "Look, this is the guy that I've been telling ya'll about, He's about to change the game, fellas." John is pointing his disciples to Jesus as the redeemer. He is not called *a lamb*, but *THE Lamb*. In addition, "the Lamb" is called "God's Lamb."

Usually, in the Bible, the possession of a lamb is from the perspective of a human being who offers an animal to God for the atonement of sin. But in this case, Jesus is depicted as the Lamb offered on our behalf. Jesus is the one—The Lamb—who will satisfy the pending wrath that hovers over us because of sin's grip. Moreover, this Lamb is the definitive sacrifice that will end the need for other sacrifices to be made. Hebrews 10:4 says, "For it is impossible for the blood of bulls and goats to take away sins." This lets us know that all of the sacrifices that have been made never took away sins. Although God valued them—in that their sacrifice was a sign of obedience—they didn't act as an eternal propitiation for our sins.

God brought Jesus as the ultimate sacrifice for us. Ultimately, all previous sacrifices pointed to Jesus who would remove sin.

For lower and middle class households, there is something called "layaway." Layaway holds a valuable item for very little currency until the full payment for that item is made. Once the full balance is paid, the desired item is released from hold—in other words, the item is redeemed. Our lives were put on hold through the blood of bulls and goats, but the funding wasn't enough to pay for our sins in full. Therefore, Jesus came to take our lives off layaway.

In light of this, when Jesus *walked by* in John 1, we see that He, as the Lamb of God, is the walking embodiment of grace. In essence, Jesus is our redemption, the purchase of something that had been lost, by the payment of a ransom.[2] Our ransom isn't from Satan, but from the wrath of God (Rom. 5:9).

One of my favorite hymns that exemplifies this says:

> *O come, o come, Emmanuel, And ransom captive Israel,*
> *That mourns in lonely exile here, Until the Son of God*
> *appear. Rejoice! Rejoice! Emmanuel Shall come to thee, O*
> *Israel.*

The debt against us is not viewed as cancelled, but as fully paid—an important distinction. Christ's blood and life, which He surrendered for them, is the "ransom" by which His people are delivered from the servitude of sin (and its penal consequences) and are secured. Hodges makes a strong statement on this point.

> It is the plain doctrine of Scripture that "Christ
> saves us neither by the mere exercise of power, nor by his
> doctrine, nor by his example, nor by the moral influence
> which he exerted, nor by any subjective influence on his

people, whether natural or mystical, but as a satisfaction to divine justice, as an expiation for sin, and as a ransom from the curse and authority of the law, thus reconciling us to God by making it consistent with his perfection to exercise mercy toward sinners."[3]

Jesus walking by was more significant than any other human walking by; it was God in the flesh uncloaking heaven's grace. We must recognize that grace still walks by us. It is a beacon for us to see grace through Jesus Christ.

I remember grace beaconing me November 15, 1992, on the campus of the great Bowie State University (HBCU). I heard for the first time the call of grace through a small campus ministry service that cold Sunday morning. I was scheming on a young lady and we went together, holding hands, to this service. Like never before, as the evangelist proclaimed the grace of God in Jesus Christ, I found myself drawn to an aroma I hadn't smelled before. It was confusing because it was both attractive and confrontational. In what was seemingly a conflict of interests, was the drawing power of God giving me eyes to recognize grace walking by.

Even creation points its ecological finger, through its role as a preacher, toward God's existence (Rom. 1:20). It moves man toward the road of belief and surrender. Just as it points—as it preaches—we who are in Christ proclaim God's favor in the person of Jesus Christ. All cross paths with grace, but not all respond to it. We will explore ways we cross paths with the grace of God.

Follow Jesus?

If anyone knows me, they know that I am a student and lover of soul, R&B, hip-hop, gospel, and jazz music. In a word: I love culture. I am an avid student of the lives that hip-hop artists lead. I study where they came from, their influences, what shapes their expression, the nature of those they attract as fans, and those who hang in their entourages. Hip-hop entourages seem to be different than other artists.

These crews are made up of friends and family who are a part of the trusted inner circle of the artist. They live off the artist's success and have an unbridled personal loyalty to the artist (sometimes) and the artist's interests. Crew loyalty runs so deep that what ever the artist is for, they are for. Whomever the artist is against, they are against. Wherever the artist goes, they go. Their lives are explicitly tied to the career of that artist. If the artist falls, they fall. If the artist has success, they ride the artist's wave up in life.

Following Jesus has some parallels to hip-hop crews. The disciples of Jesus were driven by a loyalty to the interests of God revealed through Jesus Christ. Following Jesus is a foundational concept in the Synoptics, especially in the Gospel of John. Following Jesus is synonymous with the concept of discipleship. The verb "followed" is in the tense that indicates a once-for-all action, which may mean that they cast in their lot with Jesus.[4] We should also notice that the verb has both a general sense of "follow" and a more specific sense of "follow as a disciple." The disciples walked down the path after Jesus and thus became literal followers. But they also symbolically committed themselves to Him.[5]

The tense[6] also points to a particular time in their lives where they decided to follow Jesus. In all of our lives we should be able to point to an encounter with grace in which we were signaled to follow the Son of God. There must be a point in our lives where we decide we are committing our lives fully to the master. At that point it marks the transformation that is unforgettable. Encounters like that mark our journey with clarity that we have met our master. The Christian life is filled with things that will seek to deter us from following Jesus.

This "following" concept will serve as a metaphor in the Gospels for discipleship. They turned their loyalty from John to Jesus. In rabbinic culture, disciples walked behind those whom they followed as teacher. They would literally follow their master around imitating him. By following Jesus, they were communicating their willingness to submit to Him as their leader. Following Jesus always means abandoning something else that preoccupied our lives prior to grace passing by and being preoccupied by Him. To follow Jesus is to follow the grace of God. This glorious abandonment changes everything. Köstenberger states,

> What is more, these early followers of Jesus show paradigmatically that with the appearance of Jesus the Messiah, those identified with old-style Judaism—even if part of a renewal movement such as the Baptist's—must leave their old religious system and associations behind for the sake of following the Messiah, Jesus. This is as relevant today as it was when the Gospel was first written and read (Burge 2000: 75).[7]

The term *follow* which occurs here for the first time in John, is used in all four Gospels with reference to Jesus' disciples.[8] Disciples in that day literally "followed" or walked behind the one whom they chose as their teacher (e.g., Hag 1. 2.1).[9] In John's gospel, however, the term gradually moves from literal to a more figurative sense, denoting a "following" of Jesus' teaching (8:12; 10:4–5, 27; 12:26; 21:19, 20, 22).[10] It is possible that the Evangelist is playing with both meanings: at one level, these two men were "following" Jesus in the most literal of senses, but at another they were taking the first steps of genuine discipleship.[11]

Disciple Defined

A disciple of Jesus Christ is one who has renounced himself or herself and pledged to being in a lifetime apprenticeship with the Lord Jesus Christ (Matt. 10:39). One who is unequivocally committed to Jesus and His goals for his or her life and His goals as seen in transforming the world (Eph. 2:10). One whose life goal is to be conformed to the image of Jesus (Rom. 8:29).

There needs to be a community of mimickers of Jesus Christ. In Jesus' day, gifted students would listen to various rabbis and approach one, chosen rabbi and ask, "May I follow you?" In effect, the student was asking, "Do I have what it takes to be like you?" The rabbi would either accept the student as a *talmid*, or would encourage him to pursue a trade. Jesus broke this pattern when He chose His own *talmidim*. As He asked His disciples to follow Him, they knew without a doubt that their rabbi believed in them. And as they came to see Jesus as the Messiah, they realized that God believed in them too.

A *talmid* did not merely follow a rabbi as a student. They desired to gain the rabbi's knowledge, but for a greater goal they wanted to become like the rabbi himself.

- A *talmid* followed the rabbi everywhere.
- Every day, and every hour of the day—often without knowing or asking where the rabbi was going.
- The *talmid* rarely left his rabbi's side for fear that he would miss a teachable moment.
- He watched the rabbi's every move, noting how he acted and thought about a variety of situations.
- *Talmidim* trusted their rabbi completely.

What Do You Want for Real for Real?

Growing up in the Mason household—around so many older folks—helped me earn a certain reputation: I was "a young old man." I loved the environment, being a fly on the wall for so many interesting discussions (many of which I'm not sure I should have heard). One of the things that was funny about being around older folks is when they talked to us, they spoke in what I would have expressed back then as a "code."

This "code" was made up entirely of questions. They would answer my questions with questions all of the time.

"What did I say?"

"Didn't I tell you?"

"Don't let me again?"

"Oh, no you didn't?"

"What do you think I'd say to that, Eric?"

"Open your mouth one more time?"

"Didn't I tell you to stay out of grown folk's conversations?"

Those were routine questions where I grew up. Their questions, when stated in this context, implied an answer that I should have known from past experiences. Those past experiences trained me to understand the "code."

Jesus' questions in the Gospels are some of the most riveting ones that we could come across. Working through His questions alone could be its own work. They could make an incredible sermon series. As I have His questions, these are some of my favorites (and the most challenging to my walk):

Matthew 20:22: But Jesus answered, "You don't know what you're asking. Are you able to drink the cup that I am about to drink?"

Mark 8:27: Jesus went out with His disciples to the villages of Caesarea Philippi. And on the road He asked His disciples, "Who do people say that I am?"

Mark 9:12: "How then is it written about the Son of Man that He must suffer many things and be treated with contempt?"

Mark 11:30: "Was John's baptism from heaven or from men? Answer Me."

Mark 12:37: "David himself calls Him 'Lord'; How then can the Messiah be his Son?"

Luke 18:19: "Why do you call Me good?" Jesus asked him. "No one is good but One—God."

John 3:10: "Are you a teacher of Israel and don't know these things?"

John 5:6: When Jesus saw him lying there and knew he had
already been there a long time, He said to him, "Do you want
to get well?"

It is estimated that Jesus' questions recorded in the Gospels
amount to about 173 in number. All of them reflect a broad range of
issues that get to the heart of those who are on the receiving side of
His communication. The Master's questions are just as riveting now
as they were to His contemporaries. Jesus' questions engage topics
in contemporary life issues now just as He did in His day—issues
such as prosperity and personal happiness, authentic belief, legalism,
betrayal, sexuality, mercy, guilt, forgiveness, and most important
of all, His identity. In light of the offer that Jesus makes to those
who are drawn to Him, the most important question is who Jesus
is (identity), why are we drawn to Him, and what it is that Jesus
actually offers.

In rabbinic culture, disciples were seen following their rabbi
everywhere. The disciples walking behind Jesus out in public was
normal for followers of a master teacher. Students would mimic
every aspect of their teacher while they were following them
through life. One writer states,

> Like other rabbis of his day, Jesus had disciples called
> talmidim, devout followers who were probably in their
> mid-teens.
>
> Gifted students approached a rabbi and asked, "May
> I follow you?" in effect, saying, "Do I have what it takes
> to be like you?" The rabbi either accepted the student as a
> talmid or sent him away to pursue a trade. Jesus broke this
> pattern when he chose his own talmidim. As he asked his

disciples to follow him, they knew without a doubt that their rabbi believed in them.

A talmid followed the rabbi everywhere, often without knowing or asking where he was going. He rarely left his rabbi's side for fear that he would miss a teachable moment. And he watched the rabbi's every move, noting how he acted and thought about a variety of situations.

Talmidim trusted their rabbi completely. They worked passionately to incorporate the rabbi's actions and words into their lives. The disciples' deepest desire was to follow their rabbi so closely that they would start to think and act like him.

Jesus' twelve disciples ultimately succeeded in becoming like their rabbi: Their missionary efforts changed the world, and most of them gave their lives in the process.[12]

A. C. Myers affirms this, connecting the Jewish idea of the *talmid* or *talmidim* to *mathetes,* a.k.a. a disciple:

A student or follower. As used in the New Testament, the English term (from Lat2. *discipulus* "pupil") reflects the Greek sense of the disciple as an adherent to the teachings of a particular teacher or school of thought (John 9:28; cf. Matt. 22:16); the followers of John the Baptist are thus identified as disciples (e.g., Mark 2:18; John 1:35, 37). To an extent, the function of the disciple is similar to that of the rabbinical talmîdîm (cf. 1 Chr. 25:8; RSV "pupil"), who studied the Law under the guidance of a particular teacher; however, akin to the alternate Greek sense of the disciple as an apprentice, these students themselves sought to gain ordination as teachers.[13]

What a profound understanding of the first-century idea of a disciple! A disciple would have wanted to learn about Yahweh from the perspective of the rabbi to whom they submitted as a learner.

Just observing the posture of a first-century disciple toward their Rabbi reveals a stark difference between how we communicate discipleship in our day from a gospel perspective. Jesus states, ultimately, that He chose them; they didn't choose Him. Jesus changes the normal pattern between student and teacher by choosing the student and choosing those who wouldn't normally be on the radar of any rabbi in His day.

However, true to form, Jesus wasn't impressed with a cultural approach to discipleship. Jesus demanded their whole life.

"What are you looking for?"[14] The question is both probing and challenging, revealing something about both the identity of the questioner and the questioned. Considering, the Fourth Evangelist's penchant for double entendre, it is hard to believe that the question is not, on a secondary level, meant to challenge also the readers of John's gospel to ask themselves what it is they are looking for.[15]

Jesus asks this question to those who would seek to follow Him: "What do you want, for real for real?" This urban idiom has embedded in it the notion that there is discontinuity between what is being sought and what will be received. Therefore, the question beckons them to consider, "So you wanna be My disciple?" with the tone of "You don't know what you want."

Following Jesus comes with glorious promises, some of which we can expect now and others which won't come to pass until the eschaton. Having an over-realized eschatology in the communication of the gospel of justification could shipwreck the faith of people. An under-realized eschatology robs believers of hope. Jesus' question paints a comprehensive picture of what it means to follow Him.

In essence, that is why the prosperity gospel is such danger, because it creates dangerous expectations in the heart of the person who places their faith in what God can give monetarily instead of the finished work of Jesus Christ on the cross. If God doesn't do it (which He won't, in many cases), it undermines the glory of God because it overemphasizes what God "can deliver on," versus the most valuable thing He has already offered—deliverance from His holy wrath.

Jesus in the course of His journey with these men throughout His incarnation and post incarnation by the Spirit and through others would deliver a finished canon filled with paradoxical promises that is sustaining for a grace-filled life. Being in a relationship with Jesus Christ by faith helps us to know what we should expect from Him. *A walk with Christ Jesus is a constant collision of human and divine expectations.* In this collision, the hope is that His will would prevail in us.

These New Testament paradoxical promises for the disciple paint a full-bodied picture of an authentic Christian life:

Mark 8:35–36: "For whoever wants to save his life will lose it, but whoever loses his life because of Me and the gospel will save it. For what does it benefit a man to gain the whole world yet lose his life?"

Mark 9:35: "If anyone wants to be first, he must be last of all and servant of all."

Luke 9:23: Then He said to them all, "If anyone wants to come with Me, he must deny himself, take up his cross daily, and follow Me."

Luke 18:29–30: So He said to them, "I assure you: There is no one who has left a house, wife or brothers, parents or children because of the kingdom of God, who will not receive many times more at this time, and eternal life in the age to come."

And this is the promise that covers them all:

2 Corinthians 1:20: For every one of God's promises is "Yes" in Him. Therefore, the "Amen" is also spoken through Him by us for God's glory.

As seen throughout the life of the disciples, their motivation for following Jesus was tested in every sense of the word . . .

- Economic turmoil
- Popularity decline
- Persecution
- Loneliness
- Viewed as disregarders of the customs of men
- Cult leaders
- Being on a fool's errand

But the promises of God guide us down the pathways of grace in a broken and confusing world. As we experience God's promises, the Spirit guides us into truth and shapes what we should expect from the Lord. Therefore, the heart of Jesus guides our expectations—not our personal preferences, unfiltered and unchallenged. Over and over again, in our lives, our humanity will collide with His divinity. At the end of the day, a disciple must be transformed into wanting what the Lord wants for them. Will you live with the challenge of following Him, as His *talmid*, while you struggle to understand grace from a divine perspective? Will you beat God to the punch? Will you follow Him?

2

EXPERIENCING GRACE

I believe in Christianity as I believe that
the sun has risen: not only because I see it,
but because by it I see everything else.
—C. S. LEWIS, *THE WEIGHT OF GLORY*

I come from a quasi-Baptist/Charismatic ("Bapticostal") background. Those who discipled me were biblically and theologically driven, but due in large part to the charismatic influence,
experience was highly valued in the framework of the Christian life.
Both theological reflection and experiencing what was illustrated
in the Bible were paramount among my disciplers. With this came
some good, but there were also some challenges.

Later in life, these challenges provoked me to deaden my ears
and heart to experiences within the faith. I overreacted; I developed
a reductionist philosophy of Christian experience that was centered
on devotional intellect and stoic application. Consequently, my worship lacked fervor in gatherings and lacked a proper theology of how
the gospel forms and transforms emotions.

As I matured in the faith, I realized that some of what was taught—and even experienced—early in life wasn't all unsound. God began breaking down the walls I built between my heart and my mind so that I could have the full experience of the faith that we all need.

Come and See

It reminds me of a season of my life when, if a song didn't have 808s (a.k.a. heavy bass) pumping out of it, the song would not have been as robust to me. One day, I wandered into a Bose store. If you've never been to a Bose store, they regularly do demonstrations of their audio systems. We went into a room in the rear of the store, and they gave an elaborate lecture on the history on their technology. The staff, after the educational portion of the presentation, began demonstrating the different types of speakers—everything from tweeters to subwoofers. I began to hear sounds that I hadn't heard before coming from movies I had seen a hundred times. I realized how much I was missing, because I only wanted subs, I only wanted the 808s, but not the other subtleties that make sound full-bodied.

In John 1:38, some disciples followed Jesus asking, "Where are You staying?" In other words, "Rabbi, we need time to talk." When people call Jesus teacher—although, as we have already seen, rabbi is common too—they do so in order to indicate "great one." The disciples are speaking to Jesus with a humble posture.

The disciples ask their teacher where He is staying. Staying is similar to the word *abiding* or *remaining*. John uses the term to indicate intensive fellowship. "Staying" is translated as one of John's characteristic words, the Greek *meno*. Here it means to reside, but it often has theological connotations of continuing on, especially in an intimate relationship.

These men may have already been wondering if that type of intimate relationship with Jesus might be possible for them. This word *meno* occurs 112 times in the New Testament, and John used it 66 of those times (40 times in his gospel). Asking such indirect questions—what they really wanted was to come home with Him—was culturally appropriate in ancient Israel. They were operating in conjunction with principles of politeness and hospitality. The "tenth hour" would be about 4 p.m., possibly too late in the afternoon to walk a long way home before dark and thus implying that a hospitable person would invite them to spend the night.[16]

In John 1:39, after being asked where He was staying, Jesus replies, "Come and you'll see." Jesus' answers are just as profound as His questions. Jesus wasn't just inviting them to see where He was staying, He was saying, "Come to me and you will see for real for real." When we follow Jesus, we always get more than we bargain for. In a later chapter we will talk about John 1:51 and see the expansiveness of Jesus' offer to "come and see."

Jesus welcomes us to investigate who He is. He welcomes both skeptics and those with hyper assumptions regarding His invitation to come and see. Jesus welcomes all types of people to understand His identity. He invites blacks, whites, Asians, Latinos, poor, rich, middle class, broken, bruised, confused, sexually deviant, prideful, urban, rural, and suburbanite people to investigate the claims concerning Him. At His incarnation Jesus called religious skeptics, businessmen, Hebrew fundamentalists, a thief, thugs, a shady government worker, a radical Jew, mama's boys, spoiled rich kids, prostitutes, demon possessed folks, religious outcasts, legalists, the licentious, physically dead, blind, leprous, and many more into one crew to represent Him. Since He is the embodiment of grace, Jesus is inviting these men to ultimately have an experience with the grace of God in and through Him.

What Is Grace: Five Aspects of God's Grace

In order to beat God to the punch, we must understand what grace is, and what grace is not.

First, grace is rooted in who God is. Grace has been rightly defined by many as "unmerited favor" (Eph. 2:8–9). This definition is true, but doesn't capture the full picture of what grace is. We see it both in the call to discipleship, "follow Me," and the call to investigate His identity, "come and see." Grace is one of the attributes that make Him God. The triune God—the Father, the Son, and the Holy Spirit—shares in this.

Second, this grace is rooted in God's loving-kindness. The *hesed/ chesed* of God found in *tanahk*, God's loving-kindness. His loving-kindness is His desire to allow humanity to experience and know who His is. Because of sin, this *chesed* is unable to be experienced in its fullest sense by all people, although God does show general loving-kindness to all creation (Matt. 5:45). Its fullest sense is only experienced by those who trust in Jesus (Eph. 2:8–9). Jesus wants us, as we seek to understand who He is, not merely to answer a list of our questions, but to invite us to *experience* His grace in the process. Then, as our questions are answered, He draws us into proper relationship with who He is. Grace, as loving-kindness, is not merely intellectual, but something we experience according to God's generous nature.

Third, grace came as a Person. One of the greatest passages on grace is Titus 2:11. Paul describes who grace is to Titus, one of his apostolic delegate church planting partners:

> For the grace of God has appeared with salvation for all people.

In the coming of the Jesus, grace appeared. In the hypostatic event, whereby Jesus merged His eternal deity into temporal humanity, grace was embodied. His appearing was a demonstration of God's loving-kindness toward humanity. This Epiphany of grace marked a change in history—men would finally experience, in the person of Jesus, the grace of God foretold by the prophets. The gospel is the unveiling of the Word, whereby Jesus taught us concerning the grace of the Yahweh.

My grandmother traveled a lot in the ninety years of her life. As she traveled, she would always bring a souvenir home from the places she visited. Whether it was a button, a plate, or a T-shirt, she wanted to prove that she went where she said she went. As a matter of fact, she would display this on her tabletop vinyl record player in the living room. The display caused many conversations between those who were drawn in by her display. In the same way, grace came in the revealed person of Jesus Christ, about whom we see so many conversations in John's gospel. It is key to know that grace, the Person, brought a heavenly souvenir with Him: salvation. This souvenir was to affirm from whom and from where He came. "Bringing salvation for all men" lets us know that He brought with Him the ability to experience a relationship with God.

Fourth, grace symbolizes something that was withheld from us.
On this point in particular, grace is often misunderstood. It is
misunderstood because many, as sinners apart from Christ, don't
recognize that something bad was in store for us. Grace is magni-
fied in the fact that God's wrath was withheld from us. Romans
5:9 states:

> Much more then, since we have now been declared
> righteous by His blood, we will be saved through Him
> from wrath.

The grace of God found in the person of Jesus Christ saved us
not merely from sin, death, hell, and the devil, but also from the
wrath of God. When we recognize that we have been saved from
God Himself and His unleashed, righteous anger toward sin, it
makes us see grace in a totally different light.

This might be the place where you put this book down and
lift your hands and worship the living God. Knowing that apart
from grace, that eternity under His wrath (as a consequence for
your sin debt) was your destiny, helps us get a fuller picture of the
grace of God. Just like a Bose stereo amplifies every audible fre-
quency, understanding how the cross provides a way for us to avoid
the wrath of God projects our understanding of grace in surround
sound.

In Jesus, the embodiment of grace, we see that on the cross the
fullness of God's wrath (as the hymn writer says) is satisfied. Praise
be to God!

Finally, Grace is the means by which we respond to God. As a
rule, grace emphasizes what God in Christ has done for us; this is
true. In God doing for us, there is an appropriate response to grace

as well. Grace can't be earned, but grace motivates and empowers us to work. These works don't merit greater favor, but they come about because of the favor of God. There are varying levels of grace at work in all of us, but one thing is consistent in all believers regarding good works: it is all by the grace of the living God.

> For *by the grace given to me,* I tell everyone among you not to think of himself more highly than he should think. Instead, think sensibly, as God has distributed a measure of faith to each one. (emphasis added)

> According to the *grace given to us,* we have different gifts. (Rom. 12:3, 6, emphasis added)

> *According to God's grace that was given to me, I have laid* a foundation as a *skilled master builder,* and another builds on it. But *each one must be careful how he builds on it.* (1 Cor. 3:10, emphasis added)

> But *by God's grace* I am what I am, and His grace toward me was not ineffective. However, *I worked more than any of them, yet not I, but God's grace that was with me.* (1 Cor. 15:10, emphasis added)

> We want you to know, brothers, *about the grace of God granted to the churches of Macedonia:* During a severe testing by affliction, their abundance of joy and their deep poverty overflowed into the wealth of *their generosity.* I testify that, *on their own, according to their ability and beyond their ability.* (2 Cor. 8:1–3, emphasis added)

> And God is able to *make every grace overflow to you,* so that in every way, always having everything you need, *you may excel in every good work.* (2 Cor. 9:8, emphasis added)

These are just a few of the many verses that extol grace as the motivation for good works. Grace is a powerful conduit for the glory and power of God through the brokenness of humanity. We understand that justification isn't possible by works, nor is any aspect of sanctification or glorification (Eph. 2:8–9; Rom. 5:1; Gal. 3:1–10; 2 Thess. 1:11–12). Those who base their relationship with God on what they have done for God might just hear something like this familiar passage:

> "Not everyone who says to Me, 'Lord, Lord!' will enter the kingdom of heaven, but only the one who does the will of My Father in heaven. On that day many will say to Me, 'Lord, Lord, didn't we prophesy in Your name, drive out demons in Your name, and do many miracles in Your name?' Then I will announce to them, 'I never knew you! Depart from Me, you lawbreakers!'" (Matt. 7:21–23)

They based their entrance into the kingdom on their work for God instead of Jesus' work on their behalf. With that perspective, even the best works would be seen as false, because they don't flow from the grace of God. With that being said, sanctification is the only aspect of our relationship with God that God demands our participation. Note an important distinction: our sanctification does not depend on our participation (it depends entirely on God's participation), but God demands that we participate. In our spiritual growth, or our sanctification,[17] we are called to work, and that work flows from what God has done for us in Jesus Christ.

For example, remember Philippians 2:12: "work out your own salvation with fear and trembling." Paul even talks about this in his own life:

Therefore I do not run like one who runs aimlessly or box like one beating the air. Instead, I discipline my body and bring it under strict control, so that after preaching to others, I myself will not be disqualified. (1 Cor. 9:26–27)

Colossians 1:29 is my favorite verse on grace-based works:

I labor for this, striving with His strength that works powerfully in me.

In essence, the whole of our walk is a work of grace.

Even in glorification—in which Jesus will culminate the fullness of our salvation by completing the work of what He secured on the cross—sanctification is the means by which grace's effects on us are brought to practical completion (2 Cor. 5:1–5). Consequently, Jesus urges us to store up treasures to be experienced in our glorified state (Matt. 6:19–21).

Even Jesus' works flowed from the same place in the Incarnation, from grace. John writes, "Let us know that all of His life was filled with or controlled by grace and truth" (John 1:14). Hebrews 5:9 shows us that Jesus progressively grew in grace-based works, "After He was perfected, He became the source of eternal salvation for all who obey Him." If our Lord's works progressively developed, flowing from grace, how much more do ours need to reflect the same reality?

Expanding the Invitation

I consider myself a movie buff. I am especially fond of movies that are based on heroic, mythical characters. I am a geek when it comes to characters from great literature. For example, I have certain "authenticity" requirements that I use for evaluation when a new movie is released. Whether it's a historic figure based on our past, or a superhero like Superman, Batman, etc., I want to see a beastly portrayal of the character(s) that I have admired in my leisure. My rationale is that authentic portrayals allow others to enjoy and experience what I experienced when I read about them. How frustrating is it when the book is better than the movie?

In John 1:40–42, the disciples' experience with Jesus was so exciting that it became contagious. They were motivated to talk to their circle of influence about the heroic character, now come to life, called *Messiah*. It isn't recorded what their evening with Jesus was like, but it is clear that it was an impactful time. In the same way that we might go on and on about the new *Avengers* movie, they go tell their closest associates.

I love the wording of the first part of verse 41, the middle of 41 and the beginning of 42: *"He first found . . . we have found . . . He brought Him to Jesus."* These statements deeply reflect the contagious excitement that flows from an authentic and gracious experience with the Lord Jesus Christ. An encounter with Jesus Christ changes everything. When you experience Jesus for who He is, you cannot help but run to your circles of influence and engage them with the one who changes everything.

I remember when music went digital. It blew my mind that CDs would possibly become obsolete like eight-track, vinyl, and tapes. The digital flow of music will forever change how we experience music. In 2004, everyone was talking about how much music they had access to on Napster. Even though digital file sharing nearly upended the recording industry, something positive and unprecedented was happing in the music business: consumers were talking about music. Of course, when iTunes began, there was a more credible response from the music industry when music went digital. Transitioning to this digital platform changed music forever.

In the same way, Jesus changes the game. When we authentically experience the Lord Jesus, we become contagious. We are then willing to spread the experience of grace. Spreading it in our families, with friends, appropriately in the workplace, and in our communities. Sadly, we as believers aren't often known for our grace, we are more broadly known for our stances on curtain "issues." There is nothing wrong with standing for truth, because Jesus was full of both grace and truth. Grace and truth are bound up in a delicate balance.

Truth lets people know where you stand, but grace lets people know you love them. How else could Jesus call Peter "Satan," and then embrace Him at the end of His earthly ministry? How else could Peter deny Jesus three times, and never bring it up again after Peter radically repented? And in contrast to Peter, why would the son of perdition (Judas Iscariot) regret—not repent—of his betrayal of the Lord? He knew that Jesus was a man of truth and grace. Grace creates an environment for truth to be heard and either accepted or rejected.

Truth makes grace clearer, and grace clarifies the offense of truth. John shows us that to see and experience grace and truth is to behold the glory of God (John 1:14a). Jonathan Edwards states it so eloquently:

Thus the disciples were assured that Jesus was the Son of God, "for they beheld his glory, as the glory of the only begotten of the Father, full of grace and truth," John 1:14. When Christ appeared in the glory of his transfiguration to his disciples, with that outward glory to their bodily eyes, which was a sweet and admirable symbol and semblance of his spiritual glory, together with his spiritual glory itself, manifested to their minds; the manifestation of glory was such, as did perfectly, and with good reason, assure them of his divinity; as appears by what one of them, viz., the Apostle Peter, says concerning it, 2 Pet. 1:16, 17, 18, "For we have not followed cunningly devised fables, when we made known unto you the power and coming of our Lord Jesus Christ, but were eyewitnesses of his majesty. For he received from God the Father, honor and glory, when there came such a voice to him from the excellent glory, This is my beloved Son, in whom I am well pleased. And this voice which came from heaven we heard, when we were with him in the holy mount." The apostle calls that mount, the holy mount, because the manifestations of Christ which were there made to their minds, and which their minds were especially impressed and ravished with, were the glory of his holiness, or the beauty of his moral excellency; or, as another of these disciples, who saw it, expresses it, "his glory, as full of grace and truth."[18]

Grace and truth are the key ingredients for God to be glorified and therefore, unleashing the contagious nature of the gospel.

Doing ministry in the city for me has been extremely rewarding, fun, painful, educational, and challenging at the same time. Not for the reasons you might think. I can remember earlier in our ministry in North Philadelphia when I was less knowledgeable of who was in our neighborhood, the changing demographics, and the differing sociological backgrounds of our people. Listening back at some of the sermons from that time is beyond painful for me.

I didn't realize how much I needed to soften a tone that was rooted, not in Scripture, but in wanting to be accepted by the "more sound," "theologically solid," and "exegetically rigorous" spheres of Western Christianity. We had (and have) as neighbors practicing gay and lesbians, black nationalists, atheists, abortion recipients, drug addicts, bootleg entrepreneurs, Ivy League folks, church hurt people, etc., and the list goes on. We experienced a great deal of transiency, as a result of being in a place that people don't look to move to or raise their family. Our neighborhood needed truth that was seasoned by grace.

On the other hand, I believe that God works even when we unknowingly mismanage opportunities to proclaim truth with grace. The Lord was gracious in so many ways despite me, but I am learning to be more aware of the role that grace plays in the life of people from diverse backgrounds.

I can remember one Sunday when I was preaching, I saw a young lady in the congregation whose appearance was very masculine. I spontaneously brought up homosexuality (the message and text was far from that topic), and I was immediately grieved because

I bruised the young lady who had been coming to the church for several weeks.

At the end of the service, after I said "amen" at the benediction, she made a beeline for me. She expressed her frustration with, not my bringing up homosexuality, but with the way I handled the situation. I immediately repented. I didn't repent for what I believed (the truth about biblical sexuality), but for the way I conveyed it to someone who was being drawn into our community. We never saw her again after that week. To this day my soul grieves that situation.

Later, many more came and the Lord is teaching me how to graciously engage not only homosexuals, but fornicators, liars, the greedy, and others with truth. The apostle Paul in 1 Corinthians 6:11 describes it like this: "And some of you used to be like this." Many have come to Jesus, and in the midst of it I have found grace to be so amazingly contagious. In light of this shift, God has used that situation to change the spirit of the church into a more gracious community, for which I am ecstatic!

Grace, in many respects, is the incarnation of hope. Paul points to this in Romans 15:1–13. Grace is not mentioned explicitly in the passage, but it is present implicitly. Without grace, there can be no hope. Expressing to people that God is after them to love and save them changes everything.

Grace Potential

Speeches or sermons that come off as motivational irritate me. Motivational "talks" always seem disingenuous. The whole "you can do it" type of messages don't work for me. I know people need encouragement—of course. But true encouragement doesn't ignore the brokenness, hurt, and hopelessness that haunt the lives of so many. Grace is God's work of creating potential where there is none, in spite of our circumstances.

In preaching, there is a very fine line we need to walk in our messages. Pragmatism, in so far as it relates to biblical application, has its place, but on its own pragmatism will leave us depending on our own works rather than on what Christ has already done. Theological depth is important; it helps us know who God is, who we are in Him, and how we ought to live our lives. In preaching, we walk the thin line of helping people while holding all three of these aspects in proper balance. If we over (or under) emphasize any of the three—knowledge about God, focus on self, or Christian living—our lives will suffer. Focus on self will lead toward valuing the gospel message like consumer benefits. What do I get? What's in it for me? On the other hand, theological knowledge can enrapture a person's mind, but fail to help them walk with God. Therefore, we must help people to understand who God is, who we are, and how to walk according to God's will in light of God's grace.

Jesus meets Peter for the first time in John 1:42 and says, "'You are Simon, son of John. You will be called Cephas' (which means 'Rock')." Christ's statement is an interesting one, because Peter was far from being anything close to a rock. Jesus hasn't taken Peter through any process. As a matter of fact, if Jesus would have named

Peter based on his accomplishments within his discipleship process, his name would be quite different.

Jesus asserts His authority by nicknaming Peter. It is a little strange to just meet someone and give them a new name. But in Old Testament times, God frequently changed people's names to indicate their special calling (e.g., Abraham, Israel). Rabbis in Jesus' day likewise occasionally gave characteristic names to their disciples. Jesus' "renaming" of Simon Peter is therefore in keeping with both biblical and rabbinic precedents.[19]

> But, says Jesus, *You will be called Cephas:* doubtless in Aramaic the expression was kêpā, a word meaning "rock." The terminal "s" in "Cephas" reflects an attempt to give the Aramaic word a Greek spelling (a pattern also adopted by Paul, e.g. 1 Cor. 9:5; Gal. 1:18). Because most of his readers cannot be expected to know any semitic language, John provides the translation, "Peter."[20]

> "Peter" does not appear to have been a proper name in ancient times. It may have been used by Jesus as a nickname[21] indicating Peter's strength of character (Ridderbos 1997: 86) and future role in the church.[22] Not that Peter is worthy of such an epithet by himself; rather, the new name is prophetic of the new man whom God would someday create (Morris 1995: 141; cf. Carson 1991: 156). The focus instead is on Jesus as the one who intimately knows people, and "so calls them that He makes them what he calls them to be" (Carson 1991: 156). This points to the "reliability of the apostolic witness . . . the historic foundations of which are laid bare here" (Ridderbos 1997: 86).[23]

In the renaming of Peter, Jesus puts His divine foreknowledge on display. Jesus foresaw what the future held for Peter—both his strengths and his weaknesses—and named him the rock anyway. Peter wasn't a rock when:

- He constantly put his foot in his mouth
- He rebuked Jesus and demanded He renounce His calling and the cross
- He committed apostasy

But Jesus is foreshadowing that one day Peter will live up to the name based on God's grace working through him. Jesus doesn't see who you are now, but He sees who you can be as a fully committed disciple fueled by gracious loyalty to Himself through Peter.

I have said it before and I'll say it again, God is the worst chooser of people in the history of humanity. Before you yell, "blasphemy," let's do inventory:

- Abraham and Sarah were well beyond the child-bearing years, but He chose them.
- Moses stuttered, but was called to speak for Him.
- David was the hidden son who even the prophet wasn't looking for and he became the greatest king in Israel and all kings' dynasties were judged by his example (in spite of his moral failures).
- Gideon was the least in the entire nation.
- Rahab was a prostitute.
- Daniel and his boys were young (and possibly eunuchs), but God used them to confound the greatest king in the known world.

All of these broken witnesses ultimately pointed to the One who wouldn't fail and is the only one whom, by His works, earned His position before. Jesus was the only one worthy of His calling; others had to be made worthy.

God picks, by grace—according to His nature, His loving-kindness, withholding His wrath—to blow the minds of men, to create potential where there is none, in order for all of the glory to go to Him.

Being in church planting and pastoral ministry, I am beginning to understand how to apply this principle in leadership development. When I look at how many of us pick leaders, sometimes we don't always pick people based on seeing God's hand on people, but our hand alone. I am now trying to come alongside leaders, searching for how the Lord is already working in their lives. One of my current elders and another son in the ministry were such men. They weren't viewed as the best candidates in the eyes of other ministry leaders. They weren't extremely vocal, they didn't verbally communicate their theological grid all the time (although they are deeply theologically rooted). But they were F.A.T.—that is Faithful, Available, and Teachable. Second Timothy 2:2 says to trust these things to "faithful men," not men who reflect our personal preferences. Now both of them are pioneering ministry in very hard places and leading scores of broken people. I find my heart proud (in a good way) of them, and I am thankful that God gave me "grace potential glasses."

The contagious work of grace gives our broken lenses the ability to see potential for what is not currently present in the lives of others. As we walk in this, people's lives are changed and the glory of God emanates from places that people wouldn't have dreamed it would. Ultimately, what makes grace contagious is Jesus and the Spirit, not us.

3

HOW GRACE WORKS

"Pilgrim (parepidmos) tells us we are people who spend
our lives going someplace, going to God, and whose
path for getting there is the way, Jesus Christ."
—EUGENE H. PETERSON, *A LONG OBEDIENCE
IN THE SAME DIRECTION*[24]

Old preachers used to say, "Whatever you need, it is in His
name." Living a grace-filled life requires us to look into the
name of Jesus and discover what we lack. When I look at the names
of Jesus, I see a buffet of grace. All the food groups of the soul are
in His name, so that our souls will never find themselves malnour-
ished. This grace buffet is for us to see that nothing we have could
have been obtained on our own.

As I engage people in my neighborhood who are more Islamic
in their persuasion with the gospel, I find the largest communicated
obstacle to the gospel is the personality of Jesus. Who Jesus is per-
ceived to be then is the challenge. They respect Him as a prophet-
teacher, they even believe that He lived a perfect life, but they

cannot imagine Him being God. Sometimes I am bewildered that I believe the gospel. When I hear them break down their seemingly "objection" unbelief, I marvel at the grace of belief. Jesus says that no one can come to Him unless the Father draws them (John 6:44). What these men are experiencing in this passage is being drawn to the Lordship of Jesus Christ by God the Father. Consequently, this is why upon Peter's climactic confession of the identity of Jesus in Matthew 16, of being "the Christ, the Son of the Living God (v. 16 ESV)," Jesus would tell Him that flesh and blood did not reveal this to Him. Names mean a ton in the economy of the living God.

Names Mean Something

It's easy to miss all of the titles the writers of Scripture use to describe Jesus. We see He is called Lamb of God, Rabbi, Messiah, Him of whom Moses in the law and also the prophets wrote, Jesus of Nazareth the son of Joseph, Son of God, and king of Israel. These are some quite complex titles. It isn't clear what they mean as they communicate each of these titles to or about Jesus, but it can be concluded that they have respect for Him.

From the first encounter with Him to the last portion of this section, we see that the more time the disciples spent with Jesus, the more their understanding of who He is progressed. The more time we spend with Jesus, the more our understanding of who He is will become clear. The more time we spend in His Word, in prayer, with the people of God, living on mission for Him, being exposed to Him in intense God-centered, cross-centered, resurrection-centered, second advent, Spirit-filled worship, His majesty becomes real. It will engage our minds and hearts and then be tested and applied in the afflictions of life. The old church used to say, "I would have never known Him as a lawyer unless I was in trouble, I would have never known Him as a healer unless I was sick, I would have never known Him as a mind-regulator unless I was losing my mind." I am 'bout to shout right now, fam, so let's move on!

These titles are all true of Jesus, but they are not mutually exclusive. None of these titles are meant to stand solo; they are meant to be a symphony of the glory of the Messiah. Let's take some time and work through the progression.

John 1:35–51 is filled with titles for Jesus. Not many sections of Scripture, especially in narrative passages, contain this number of titles. These titles are extremely important because they reflect how people perceive Him. Jesus, in Matthew 16:13–15, conducts a survey of His disciples to get a sense of who people say that He is. Jesus wasn't doing a presidential poll for Himself, but He is concerned with how those who claim to follow Him are processing through their encounters with Him.

Lamb of God is the first title in this section. John the Baptist is the first to call Jesus "Lamb of God" (John 1:29, 36). We have already engaged this idiom in a former chapter, but we will deal with it on different terms. I wonder if Jesus told the disciples that He would be the Pascal lamb (and explained it to them in Isaiah 53)? That is impossible to know; all we know is that John's statement caused two of His followers to follow Jesus and become more curious about His identity.

This passage could also point back to the fulfillment of Abraham's statement to his son Isaac.

> Genesis 22:8 is an important passage for the background of Jesus' title Lamb of God. In Jewish thought, this was held to be a supremely important sacrifice. G. Vermès

> stated: "For the Palestinian Jew, all lamb sacrifice, and
> especially the Passover lamb and the Tamid offering, was
> a memorial of the Akedah with its effects of deliverance,
> forgiveness of sin and messianic salvation" (*Scripture and
> Tradition in Judaism* [StP4B], 225).[25]

So on some level, they understood that Messiah would usher in an era of spiritual renewal. *We must recognize that there is no grace-filled life without comprehensive spiritual renewal.* This is the promise that Jesus brings to us, spiritual renewal. For these curious disciples of John, they needed more information.

No other term in this section screams the grace of God and how we experience a grace-filled life more than this idiom. Jesus, as Lamb of God, points us to the fact that we experience forgiveness and empowerment through His work on the cross. John's communication confronts the fact that Jesus will be the ultimate sacrifice. In essence, Jesus is the sacrifice of sacrifices:

> In the OT most passages referring to a lamb speak
> of sacrifice (85 out of the total of 96). Combined with
> a reference to the taking away of sin, it is difficult to see
> how a reference to sacrificial atonement is to be rejected.
> Characteristically the lamb in Scripture puts away sin by
> being sacrificed. "God's Lamb" means that this provision
> is made by God himself. A reference to sacrifice seems
> undeniable, but a connection with any one sacrifice is hard
> to make. All that the OT sacrifices foreshadowed, Christ
> perfectly fulfilled. God's Lamb puts sin away finally.[26]

Jesus is the gracious sacrifice for sin that only God could provide. Christ, that Pascal Lamb, would be the one on whom all of the wrath of God would be poured in order for us to experience His grace. Bowing the knee to Christ is the only way to seize a grace-filled life.

When they followed Jesus, they first called Him rabbi. Rabbi is first base. This is a title of respect.

> By the 1st century c.e. "rabbi" was a loose designation for a teacher, meaning "my master" or "my great one." This term appears in three of the four Gospels, typically in reference to Jesus. In Mark, only the disciples call Jesus "rabbi," and this address typically follows a miraculous event (Mark 9:5; 11:21; 14:45; "rabboni" at 10:51). In Matthew the only person to address Jesus as "rabbi" is Judas (Matt. 26:25, 49). The remainder of the disciples choose other titles. . . . In a speech by Jesus, the term seems to refer to one who is a teacher of the law (Matt. 23:7–8). Luke's gentile audience would have found little meaning in a term like "rabbi" because its origin is in the Jewish culture. In the Gospel of John "rabbi" is used by both the disciples and outsiders to designate Jesus (John 1:38, 49; 3:26; 4:31; 6:25; 9:2; 11:8). When Mary Magdalene encounters the risen Christ, she exclaims "rabbouni" (John 20:16). Twice the term is glossed with *didáskalos*, "teacher" (John 1:38; 20:16).[27]

But rabbi fails to adequately describe the eternal Son of God. When Jesus' disciples spent any amount of time with Him, their designation would shift from rabbi to a loftier title. For example, remember when Andrew went to find his brother Peter? Once he gets to him, he introduces Jesus as the Messiah. Jesus was still Peter's rabbi, but for Peter, Jesus was becoming much more than a teacher,

He was becoming for him the promised Messiah the prophets foretold.

Or take for example when Jesus finds Philip, and he becomes the only one who gets a formal invite to follow Him. Philip goes to Nathaniel and says, "We have found Him of who Moses in the law and also the prophets wrote" (John 1:45 ESV). Nathaniel is skeptical and limits that claim based on His hometown. When Nathaniel encounters Jesus, he calls Him rabbi, Son of God, and king of Israel. For the disciples, Jesus didn't remain a teacher for long; He became much more important in their lives.

My point about Jesus is this; people who truly encounter Him and people who truly respond to Him will always have their perceptions blown by Him. This is an act of grace. We seize this type of life by submitting ourselves to Him. We follow Him, we pray to Him, we experience Him through the Word, we investigate His identity, and ultimately, we bow down to Him as Savior and Lord. Living a bowed down, submitted life to the Lordship of Jesus Christ will get progressively easier as we more fully grasp who He is. The more clearly we understand and become intimately acquainted with Jesus and His identity, things in our life become clearer. Contrastingly, going through life without the one by whom all things were created, things will be foggy. Jesus created everything to be connected to His purposes. If we are detached from Him, we will be detached from His purposes (Col. 1:16), and life will get messy.

In Christ's incarnation, He came to eliminate the fog that inhibits knowing God. No one has ever seen God. The One and Only Son, the One who is at the Father's side—He has revealed Him (John 1:18). Jesus, directed by the grace of God, came to explain what God is like. He exegetes Him, if you will. Jesus' eternal relationship with the Father is revealed in His sinless life. All of the purposes of God are seen clearly through Jesus Christ.

As a pastor—in my personal life, my family life, my church and community life—I find that being clear or unclear about the identity of Jesus makes or breaks our lives. Knowing Jesus, as the revelator of the grace of God, is the most freeing thing one can experience. Knowing that He performed what I should have, so that I don't have to, is amazing! The names given to Jesus are a testimony of who He is and what He has done. John's gospel contains many of the names given to Jesus, but still is nowhere near comprehensive. These are others we find in pages of Scripture:

Adam
Advocate
Almighty
Alpha and Omega
Amen
Angel
Angel of his presence
Anointed
Apostle
Arm of the Lord
Author and perfecter of our faith
Beginning and end of the creation of God
Beloved Bishop
Blessed and only Potentate
Branch
Bread of life
Bridegroom
Bright and morning star
Brightness of the Father's glory
Captain of the Lord's army
Captain of salvation
Carpenter
Carpenter's son
Chief Shepherd
Chief corner stone
Child
Chosen of God
Christ
The Christ
Christ, a King
Christ Jesus
Christ Jesus our Lord
Christ of God
Christ, the chosen of God
Christ the Lord
Christ the power of God
Christ the wisdom of God
Christ, the Son of God
Christ, Son of the Blessed
Commander
Consolation of Israel
Corner stone
Counselor
Covenant of the people
David
Daysman
Dayspring
Day star
Deliverer

Desire of all nations
Door
Elect
Emmanuel
Ensign
Eternal life
Everlasting Father
Faithful and True
Faithful witness
Faithful and true
    witness
Finisher of faith
First and last
First begotten
First begotten of the
    dead
Firstborn
Foundation
Fountain
Forerunner
Friend of sinners
Gift of God
Glory of Israel
God
God blessed for ever
God manifest in the
    flesh
God of Israel, the
    Savior
God of the whole earth
God our Savior
God's dear Son
God with us
Good Master
Governor
Great shepherd of the
    sheep
Head of the church

Heir of all things
High priest
Head of every man
Head of the church
Head of the corner
Holy child Jesus
Holy one
Holy one of God
Holy one of Israel
Holy thing
Hope [our]
Horn of salvation
I Am
Image of God
Jehovah's fellow
Jesus Christ
Jesus Christ our Lord
Jesus Christ our Savior
Jesus of Nazareth
Jesus of Nazareth,
    King of the Jews
Jesus, the King of the
    Jews
Jesus, the Son of God
Jesus, the Son of
    Joseph
Just man
Just one
Just person
King
King of Israel
King of the Jews
King of saints
King of kings
King of glory
King of Zion
King over all the earth
Lamb

Lamb of God
Lawgiver
Leader
Life
Light
Light, everlasting
Light of the world
Light to the Gentiles
Light, true
Living bread
Living stone
Lion of the tribe of
    Judah
Lord
Lord of lords
Lord of all
Lord our righteousness
Lord God Almighty
Lord from heaven
Lord and Savior Jesus
    Christ
Lord Christ
Lord Jesus
Lord Jesus Christ
Lord Jesus Christ our
    Savior
Lord of glory
Lord of Armies
Lord, mighty in battle
Lord of the dead and
    living
Lord of the Sabbath
Lord over all
Lord's Christ
Lord, strong and
    mighty
Lord, the, our
    righteousness

Lord, your holy one
Lord, your redeemer
Man Christ Jesus
One of sorrows
Master
Mediator
Messenger of the
    covenant
Messiah
Messiah the Prince
Mighty God
Mighty one of Israel
Mighty one of Jacob
Mighty to save
Minister of the
    sanctuary
Morning star
Most holy
Most mighty
Nazarene
Offspring of David
Only begotten
Only begotten of the
    Father
Only begotten son
Only wise God, our
    Savior
Outstanding among
    ten thousand
Passover
Plant of renown
Potentate
Power of God
Physician
Precious corner stone
Priest
Prince
Prince of life

Prince of peace
Prince of the kings of
    the earth
Prophet
Propitiation
Rabbi
Rabboni
Ransom
Redeemer
Resurrection and life
Redemption
Righteous branch
Righteous judge
Righteous servant
Righteousness
Rock
Rock of offence
Root of David
Root of Jesse
Rose of Sharon
Ruler in Israel
Salvation
Sanctification
Sanctuary
Savior
Savior, Jesus Christ
Savior of the body
Savior of the world
Scepter
Second Adam
Seed of David
Seed of the woman
Servant
Servant of rulers
Shepherd
Shepherd and bishop
    of souls
Shepherd, chief

Shepherd, good
Shepherd, great
Shepherd of Israel
Shiloh
Son of the Father
Son of God
Son of Man
Son of the blessed
Son of the highest
Son of David
Star
Sun of righteousness
Surety
Stone
Stone of stumbling
Sure foundation
Teacher
True God
True vine
Truth
Unspeakable gift
Very Christ
Vine
Way
Which is, which was,
    which is to come
Wisdom
Wisdom of God
Witness
Wonderful
Word
Word of God
Word of life
Those who use his
    name must depart
    from evil[28]

And still, we could fill many more books with English, Greek, Hebrew, or Spanish words and fail to adequately describe His greatness. Human language is God's grace-filled way of condescending to our level so that we can *try* to comprehend His greatness. I like the way one hymn writer put it:

> *Could we with ink the ocean fill,*
> *And were the skies of parchment made,*
> *Were every stalk on earth a quill,*
> *And every man a scribe by trade,*
> *To write the love of God above,*
> *Would drain the ocean dry.*
> *Nor could the scroll contain the whole,*
> *Though stretched from sky to sky.*[29]

Grace Stalks Us

Nino Brown is a name that is known only to certain sectors of the world. Nino Brown is a mythical figure from the movie *New Jack City*. Wesley Snipes starred as drug dealer and crime lord Nino Brown in the 1991 film. The movie told the story of Nino's gang, the CMB, or the Cash Money Brothers, who make a fortune dealing crack cocaine in 1980s New York City. They even take over an entire apartment complex and dub it "the Carter." But one detective, played by Ice-T, is intent on busting Nino and bringing down the CMB. Nino is eventually brought to justice, but not before delivering one heck of a "don't-blame-this-drug-epidemic-on-me" speech.

One of the most memorable quotes from the movie is an ironic biblical statement by Cain to God about the killing of His brother Abel, "Am I my brother's keeper?" Nino and his would-be brother (G-money) uses it as a statement of loyalty. As the money was rolling in, they were doing extremely well. As the movie went on, it becomes clear that Nino wasn't as fully committed as he first seemed. Another competing motto that guides his life was, "It's always business, never personal." G-money made some major mistakes that cost them millions of dollars, and once this happened, CMB and being my "brother's keeper" went out the window in poetic fashion. Nino kills G-money right after he asks, "Am I my brother's keeper?" and answers, "Yes, I am."

Loyalty is a difficult thing to find in life, yet God in His grace is loyal. He shows His loyalty to us through Jesus Christ. God is so loyal to us, in fact, that He makes loyalty a benefit to all those who embrace Him as Lord and Shepherd. As disciples of Jesus Christ, He leaves us with a glorious promise at His ascension to the right hand of the Father:

"I will never leave you nor forsake you." (Heb. 13:5)

In the Lord telling us this, He is stating the enduring nature of His loyalty to us.

The Holy Spirit Dispenses God's Loyalty

The Holy Spirit is called many things, but one of my favorites is the Spirit of Grace. In Hebrews 10:29, He is called the gracious Spirit. One commentator says it could be translated, "the Spirit from whom he received grace."[30] The Spirit of God is the means by which we initially experienced the grace of God and continue to experience grace in our everyday lives. In light of this, it is an outrage when we refuse to respond to the loyalty that He has demonstrated toward us through the gospel. Another commentator help us to flesh this out more plainly.

> They insult the Spirit of grace. The full understanding of redemptive truth, the awareness that the blood of Jesus can make one holy, the pleasures of meeting together with other Christians; all have been a gracious ministry of the Holy Spirit to the individuals considered here. Now these are being rejected and treated with contempt. It is an egregious insult to the One who was sent to draw men and women to salvation. It actually means to become guilty of the sin which Jesus called "an eternal sin," unpardonable in any age (Mk 3:29).[31]

We understand that Jesus' being full of grace and truth flowed from the ministry of the Spirit of Grace active in His life. That activity was illustrated at His baptism, all the way to the end, His sacrificial death. This is rich because it shows that our Lord—in His humanity—was in deep need of the Spirit of Grace. His life showed us grace, and His death and resurrection opened the door for His grace to be imparted to us. Carson affirms this here,

> In Hebrews 9:14 our author declared that Christ offered himself to God as an unblemished sacrifice "through the eternal Spirit." In this context we suggested that, as with earlier references, readers could be expected to identify the eternal Spirit with the Holy Spirit (3:7; 6:4; 9:8; see 10:15). The adjective *eternal* suggests an eschatological dimension to the activity of the Spirit, who anointed Jesus as high priest for every aspect of his ministry, including his sacrificial death. In the light of the wider

discourse of chapters 9–10, then, the connection of the
Spirit with Christ's sacrifice may explain the mention of
the Spirit of grace here.[32] If the phrase signifies "the gracious
(i.e., grace-giving) Spirit,"[33] then our author is affirming
that he who was active in the Son's work on the cross is
the Spirit from whom God's grace was received by the
listeners. He had an active role in their initial acceptance
of salvation and confirmed for them the truth of the gospel
(2:3–4; 6:4–5). It is this gracious Spirit whom the apostate
has arrogantly *insulted*.[34]

Being filled with the Spirit also means being filled with the
grace of God. The Spirit works both inwardly and outwardly, work
made available to us through Jesus Christ—a radical display of
God's loyalty to us.

Chased by Grace

As we walk with the Lord, we find that God's commitment
to us is unending. A verse in the Bible that illustrates this is Psalm
23:6, "Surely goodness and mercy shall follow me all the days of my
life" (ESV). David, the shepherd-king, speaks of different seasons of
life in which the Lord shepherds him; He follows him like a shepherd pursues his sheep. From still waters to valleys of darkness, the
Shepherd—who is both good and merciful in His pursuit—stalks
the believer through life's ups and downs. When the writer of
Hebrews states that the Lord will "never leave you or forsake you"
(13:5), it is not a promise that started in the New Testament. It is
a carry-over from what God has stated in various ways throughout
the Scripture. The God of the Bible is the same yesterday, today,
and forever.

Goodness and mercy are both requisite to beat God to the punch by the power of the Spirit. Goodness and mercy are attributes of the living God. They are aspects of God's character that require God's willful actions to pursue us. This means that the Spirit of Grace has to cause goodness and mercy to pursue us, because these characteristics testify to whom a person belongs. This is not something we can do under our own power. Goodness here points to the unending enjoyment that God provides through all the seasons of life. Wow! It is an act of grace for us to enjoy life through both mountains and valleys. Submission to God's Lordship in seasons of brokenness, fear, and pain empowered through the Spirit aids us to find satisfaction in the Lord even in the lean and mean seasons.

Thru It All

As a pastor in the inner city, it seems as if all seasons are lean. Ministering in a broken context and being broken yourself can lead to despair. I walk over trash, homeless people, liquor bottles and beer cans, boarded-up homes, thugs, Muslims, drug strips, and hopelessness every day as I go to work at our church facility. Most days I have to pray my way to the building. For some people, this type of challenge would seem to motivate them, but if I'm honest, I find myself wrestling. The only thing that makes sense out of moving my family here for ministry is the Holy Spirit giving me satisfaction with Him, and the affirmation of my calling here seen in the transformation that the gospel is bringing to the lives of our people. As the Spirit of Grace does His work in my heart and soul, I walk those streets with the dignity of the gospel because He uses the environment to help me learn where I am really finding my satisfaction. Over time, I am learning to submit to the Lordship of the

Spirit in this matter. As this happens, I am bowing in satisfaction to the Lord as I am shown that goodness is stalking me. All of us have that as a blessed assurance.

Mercy is a beast of a term. It is that same Hebrew term of God's *hesed*. We could translate it as His loyal-love. As we have already seen, *hesed* points to God's relationship with the people or an individual, faithfulness, goodness, graciousness,[35] kindness, loving-kindness, unfailing kindness, devotion, i.e., a love or affection that is steadfast based on a prior relationship.[36] Our understanding of grace flows from this term. God's unmerited favor toward us comes from His loyalty to place His affections upon us and keep them there. That is one of the reasons that Paul prays that the Ephesian church would know the love of Christ that surpasses knowledge, that you may be filled with all the fullness of God (Eph. 3:19).

We need these assurances of grace. The reason being is that life is filled with challenging valleys that need the throttle of goodness and mercy to get through. Just because we have these assurances doesn't mean that the enemy of God falls back. It is possible for us to ignore goodness and mercy in the hard times of life. The psalmist wants us to be aware of the fact that no matter what we go through, we are being stalked by the mercy and goodness of God. Yet, the Bible also says that someone else's character stalks us—that is Satan. Satan and God's goodness and mercy don't coexist per se, but we have to choose to whose reign we will submit. Sinclair Ferguson states,

> As soon as we come to Christ, we find ourselves in territory that is full of hidden mines—sinister explosive devices planted by malignant a hand in an attempt to destroy our Christian faith.

> Of course, Satan can attack but never ultimately destroy true Christian faith, because we are preserved by grace. Therefore, he seeks to destroy our enjoyment of the grace of God. In this, sadly, he frequently succeeds.[37]

There is a need for us to draw on the grace of God from the Spirit of God through goodness and mercy. As we experience God granting us strength throughout the differing seasons of our lives, we grow in submission to the Lordship of Jesus Christ.

The old school translation says, "Yea, though I walk through the valley of the shadow of death" (Ps. 23:4 KJV). I like the fact that we don't pitch a tent in our problems, but the grace of God aids us in moving through our valleys. We were never meant to allow valleys to cause stagnancy, but we can thrive in our walk with Jesus Christ even through the most challenging of circumstances. Whether trials last a season or a lifetime, full deliverance will not come until we are with the Lord. Until then, all of our travels will have varying levels of turbulence.

It helps me to know that all of our sufferings have a beginning date and an expiration date. The role of grace is not to eliminate suffering, but to sustain us through the valley. *Goodness and mercy following us all the days of our life* in the context of the psalm displays God's loyalty, not just to us, but to His name. This should compel us to represent Him well—for the sake of His name—especially in those dark days. We will be held accountable for how we reflected the Lord's glory in every season of life, not just the days it was simple (and those days are few). Goodness and mercy pursuing us through the Spirit extinguishes all of our excuses for allowing our fervency for His Lordship to wane during hard times.

When my wife and I lost our first child, Naomi Michelle Mason, we were devastated. Talk about a valley. It was the last semester of our seminary journey and she was six months pregnant. We found out at a routine appointment that the baby had no heartbeat. We prayed and believed God for a resurrection that day. I laid my hands on her belly and tried to pray the walls of the hospital down. Scores of saints rushed in to pray for us and ask God for the same. With nothing happening, we approached the point when we had to make a decision on how we would proceed. Labor was induced. It was one of the most painful valleys we had seen to date. However, the Lord seemed to give us a strange joy and strength that was evident in our apparent weakness.

I harkened back to explain what it was that kept us in such a dark valley. To this day we think about what she would have looked like and what she would have become. There is still a bit of a sting left in all of this. However, we know that goodness and mercy were following us through that valley and will in all the ones to follow. Grace is a strange and loyal keeper of the brokenhearted in the Lord Jesus Christ. It acted like a life respirator to us. It helped us to breathe and continue living when we could not see beyond where we were. For me, this is the glory of a grace-filled life. God committing Himself to be uncloaked in circumstances that would feel like a veil to His glorious presence. Being near to the brokenhearted and those who are crushed in spirit.

The Assurance of Grace

"Surely" in the passage can be translated, "no doubt." The Eric Mason translation would read "you can bank on." At this point in the African-American church experience, as soon as the preacher says, "Surely," the church would stand to its feet to get ready to celebrate this word. It signifies a divine promise from the Lord. Everyone would stand, not as some stale form of tradition, but the people would stand to join in the celebration of our hope in the promises of the Lord. The preacher would say something like this:

> No matter how hard, surely
> No matter the situation, surely
> No matter who betrays you, surely
> In sickness, surely
> Late in the midnight hour, surely
> No matter the breath of your tears, surely
> Not matter the loss
> Through sickness, surely
> Through broken relationships, surely

I think we get the picture.

Each time God chose to send His people into the world to represent Him, He gave them some type of assurance. Assurance is a reminder from God that there are some things that we can bank on to focus us in on Him. John says assurance statements like, in 1 John 5:11–13:

> And this is the testimony: God has given us eternal life, and this life is in His Son. The one who has the Son has life. The one who doesn't have the Son of God does not have life. I have written these things to you who believe in the name of the Son of God, so that you may know that you have eternal life.

In John's gospel Jesus says, "Everyone the Father gives Me will come to Me, and the one who comes to Me I will never cast out"

(6:37). The work of the Spirit as the presence of God's grace in us affirms that we are His (Rom. 8). Therefore, we have confidence that God's grace will relentlessly pursue us. *Spiritus santuc non est skepticus*—"the Holy Spirit is not a skeptic." Martin Luther says, "The making of assertions is the very mark of the Christian. Take away assertions and you take away Christianity."[38]

Assurance reminds us that the Lord will pursue us with His goodness and mercy no matter the season. My performance doesn't merit the ability to experience God is this way; *that's not how you seize a grace-filled life*. Only Christ's finished work on the cross gives us the full benefits of the promises of God. If you want a grace-filled life, go to Him. All of the promises of God find their yes in Jesus (2 Cor. 1:20). Jesus Christ's presence in the promises of God makes God's promises truly promising. Because only through God the Son can they reach our zip code, and only through the Holy Spirit can it be delivered.

4

GRACE RECOVERED

Jesus Christ is the redemption of history. He gives it
focus—brings it under judgment—and grants it grace.
He left a throne, entered history, and found a cross!
"The word became flesh"—a piece of history—"and
tented among us." Though we be wretched—doomed
and defiled—poor and despised—through the Son
of God we have a chance to become sons of God! We
have a chance to have sonship conferred upon us! We
have a chance to be recognized as God's sons![39]

—CAESAR A. W. CLARK, SERMON

The Work of Grace throughout History

God's work of grace throughout history displays an elaborate
scheme only God could accomplish. It crosses theological lines,
geographical lines, denominational lines, ethnic and cultural lines.
Yet it has the same goal: to conform us to the image and nature of
the Lord Jesus Christ. Every single movement in history has its root

in the grace of God. Would it be now safe to say, that if a movement isn't rooted in the grace of God it may not be an authentic move of God?

Grace keeps God's people focused and causes us to make great sacrifices. A true understanding of grace doesn't lead to legalism or lawlessness, but toward a deep commitment to the Lordship of Jesus Christ and His causes. Every great leader in history who did anything great for God has had the unmerited favor of God in Christ strengthening and motivating every step of their journey.

As we look back at history since Jesus Christ came, we see things among God's people take a dark turn. From the New Testament to today, our commitment to bow to His Lordship has always distorted into confusion when His grace is misunderstood. Most of Paul's letters were written to assure or to correct either legalism or lawlessness. Both reflect a distortion of grace, just at different ends of the spectrum. Even if Paul wasn't writing to address a specific crisis, he still saw the need to proclaim the grace of God. Even to the Romans, in 6:1–2, He clarifies how grace empowers the believer to live an obedient life to the gospel.

Legalism believes that it can earn grace by obeying, on its terms, what God has said. Lawlessness believes that it doesn't matter how you live because grace cannot be earned anyway. Both fail because neither relies on God. Neither relies on grace. Neither are, as Paul says in Ephesians, "by grace, through faith" in Jesus Christ.

Rev. Dr. Caesar A. W. Clark states, "The Hebrew Christian faith is basically historical. A review of the great Jewish and Christian historians and theologians will quickly affirm the historical nature of the faith. Turning to secular historians, one finds that history is the human effort to understand one's self in the light of what has gone before."[40] History has shown that when grace does not empower one's life, there is going to be a diminished gospel legacy. In the appendix is an overview of the Lord's work at key points in history to call us back to the work of God's grace and the need for it in our lives.

Now, this summary is not exhaustive, but it is illustrative of how God uses our theology of grace to call the church back into closer relationship with Him.

In speaking about the grace of God, it is impossible to speak of those who play a prominent role in these time periods to help God's people to be called back to God's grace being the foundation for beginning and continuation of their spiritual life. Let's remember together key seasons of redemptive history.

Grace in the Early Church

St. Augustine, one of the church fathers from modern-day Algeria (Northern Africa), is sometimes called the "theologian of grace." His importance to Christian history is undeniable in every Christian tradition. Grace was a major focus of his ministry, due in large part to his commitment to carry on the legacy of the apostles. It was in the crucible of his debates with Pelagius that we see that God used his rebuttals as a mechanism throughout history for God's people to recognize the sustaining work of grace.

> Augustine's writings on grace have left an indelible mark on the history of Western Christian thought, serving as a principal resource for such diverse thinkers as Thomas Aquinas, Martin Luther and John Calvin. Augustine's most

sustained theological reflection on the subject of grace is
found in his *Anti-Pelagian* writings, penned during the
final years of his life (between AD 411–430).[41]

Many stood against Pelagius's claims that grace was not neces-
sarily needed for authentic good works. Even today we face this
challenge in debate over the necessity of the gospel to help us to
perform authentic redemptive works. Augustine's emphasis on our
need for the grace of God in all areas of life has shaped the heart
of every movement in Christian history. The battle that Augustine
fought with his pen that still bleeds into our hearts is the need for
God and a passion to submit to Him by grace.

Grace in the Reformation

The Protestant Reformation marks a point in history when
the parched souls of men felt the soothing reach of grace. Martin
Luther is often noted for being wrecked by an encounter of Romans
5:1. The apostle Paul writes under the guidance of the Holy Spirit,
"Therefore, since we have been justified by faith, we have peace
with God through our Lord Jesus Christ" (ESV). It is said that this
verse formed his understanding of salvation and might have set the
foundation for his theology of grace.

> The theology Luther discovered in the Scriptures as
> a response to the Catholic theology with which he grew
> up, was one that was filled with grace. One could look to
> any number of places in his theology to see grace at work,
> but none so prominently as his doctrine of justification.
> As Luther notes in his preface to Romans, "*Grace* and *gift*
> differ in that grace actually denotes God's kindness or

favor which he has toward us and by which he is disposed
to pour Christ and the Spirit with his gifts into us, as
becomes clear from [Romans] chapter 5, where Paul says,
'Grace and gift are in Christ, etc.' . . . God's grace is not
divided into bits and pieces, as are the gifts, but grace takes
us up completely into God's favor for the sake of Christ,
our intercessor and mediator, so that the gifts may begin
their work in us."[42]

When you read Luther, you can tell that grace was a price-
less discovery. Just like the pearl of great value in Matthew 13, he
staked the entirety of his life on progressing in its riches. Little did
he know that what was a discovery for him would change the course
of history. From the structure of the church, to political structures,
everything was shaped by Luther's arguments about the nature of
grace. The Catholic Church viewed Luther's protests as undermin-
ing the foundation of centuries of ecclesiological structures. For
them, Luther's grace was dangerous.

John Calvin is another reformer who heralded grace in his
theology. Embedded at every level is a deep sense of man's complete
dependence on God. For Calvin, grace not only saved us, but sustains every aspect of the life of the redeemed. This need for grace is
a constant state for the believer who recognizes his need for it.

Perhaps most famously, John Calvin spoke of God's
duplex gratia ("twofold grace" or "double grace"). Calvin
writes, "Christ was given to us by God's generosity, to be
grasped and possessed by us in faith. By partaking of him,
we principally receive a double grace: namely, that being
reconciled to God through Christ's blamelessness, we may
have in heaven instead of a Judge a gracious Father; and

secondly, that sanctified by Christ's spirit we may cultivate
blamelessness and purity of life."[43]

J. Todd Billings rephrases Calvin, noting that "it is
crucial to distinguish between justification and sanctification as two aspects of union with Christ—one fully
realized, and the other only partially completed. They
are inseparable for Calvin, being a 'double grace' *(duplex
gratia)* that is held together in the very person of Christ. It
is impossible to have one without the other; they do not
come in temporal stages . . . On the one hand, believers are
'passive' in receiving grace, in the sense that we add nothing to God's grace that was missing—God's grace is completely sufficient. The pardon and adoption involved in
justification is received *extra nos,* from outside ourselves."[44]

To this day, the Reformation has played a prominent role for
Christians to recognize that when grace becomes merely a footnote
in our lives and doctrine, we plunge into a place of deep darkness.
Also, what is so noticeable in the reformer's theology is the fact that
submitting to the Lordship of Jesus Christ is how grace practically
impacts one's life—it's how we *beat God to the punch,* so to speak.
It's how we seize a grace-filled life. Grace doesn't plunge us into
ruin, but rescues us from it.

As demonstrated throughout history, grace holds us accountable. It shows us where we are in our journey with God as disciples.
Recognizing our need for it and living in light of it can open up
our eyes to the blind spots that corrode our lives on every level.
During the Reformation, grace became *the* central rallying point.
No other era until then had the benevolent grace of almighty God
been so highly exalted as the centerpiece of man's relationship with

the living God. The gospel-centered movement owes much of its theological philosophy to the reformers planting the flag of grace at the center of their theological systems.

First Great Awakening

Most remember the Second Great Awakening more for its great revivals than its theological legacy. However, the First Great Awakening is more often remembered for the theological contributions made by Jonathan Edwards and George Whitefield. Their commitment to communicating grace theology has been well documented. As a matter of fact, for some, Jonathan Edwards is said to be one of the most astute thinkers by both Christians and non-Christians.

Edwards's book entitled a *Treatise of Grace* is considered a classic. It's about the nature of grace, and is his most extensive writing about the topic. "By 'grace,' Edwards refers to God's act of being gracious as well as to the reality of grace dwelling in the regenerate and the many effects of this new reality, often called 'blessings.'"[45] Whereas some Puritan theology before Edwards had limited the Holy Spirit's role to the application of God's grace, Sang Hyun Lee notes that "Grace, for Edwards, is primarily the work of the holy Spirit."[46]

Indeed, according to Edwards, "All gospel righteousness, virtue and holiness is called grace, not only because 'tis entirely the free gift of God, but because 'tis the Holy Spirit in man. . . . This grace is the Holy Spirit; because it is said, we receive of Christ's fullness, and grace for his grace [John 1:16]."[47]

Edwards's contribution of the continued work of grace in the life of the believer is deeply rooted in who we spoke of earlier, the

Spirit of Grace. As the Spirit of God dwells in the believer, so is the constant presence of the grace of God at work in us. Like Calvin, Edwards reminds us of our dependence on the grace of God. His reflections on grace are legendary. In meditating on the implications of grace, he awoke in many (me included) a deeper awareness of our need to function daily under grace's power. In many ways in Edwards's thinking, unless someone was wooed by grace in their daily life, he would not affirm their claim of experiencing the "seed of grace." He considered grace to be a seed that spreads all of the "graces" of God into the fabric of the regenerate's being. In other words, grace not only saves, but also sustains the believer.

Second Great Awakening

The Second Great Awakening could be called the practical theology era. Although theology wasn't thrown out the window per se, there was a deep push for God's people to live in light of what they knew theologically. As Douglas Sweeney states:

> Out of the Second Great Awakening—the series of revivals that filled the first third of the nineteenth century—came a coordinated effort to evangelize, liberate, and educate America's slaves. Hundreds of thousands of them responded by placing their faith in Jesus Christ, and dozens of charitable societies emerged to minister to their needs. Of course, in American social history, this is the age of important leaders such as David Walker, Denmark Vesey, Nat Turner, and Frederick Douglass, outspoken black prophets who preached the most powerfully against the sins of slavery and racism. But white evangelicals, too, made a difference among the slaves. Though often much

less bold in prophetic witness . . . they devoted count-
less hours and millions of dollars to help those living in
bondage.[48]

Charles Finney is viewed as one of the chief evangelists of this
era. He viewed the grace of God as the key to how ministry was
done in his sphere:

> Finney taught (notoriously) that "religion is the work
> of man" and that revival "is not a miracle" but "the result
> of the right use of the appropriate means." As a supernatu-
> ralist, he acknowledged that neither revival nor conversion
> ever occurs without the help of the Holy Spirit, but as an
> experienced revivalist, he claimed that these things do not
> occur without some human effort either. In the provi-
> dence of God, means are used to promote revival. Grace
> is necessary, of course, but God does not coerce the lost or
> save the spiritually complacent. Rather, grace is that which
> persuades us of the truth of Christianity. It enables anxious
> sinners to pick themselves up by their own moral boot-
> straps. It is promised to all who seek it earnestly.[49]

Finney viewed grace as God's work in salvation that annuls
the fallen nature of man, thereby aiding man to make a decision of
his own right for God. His belief in the grace of God in salvation
is sufficiently orthodox; however, many differ on the semantics of
his claim. Regardless of where you align yourself theologically, the
point is that Finney played a prominent role in communicating
grace to the people of God.

Lemuel Haynes was an older contemporary of Finney who
argued passionately against slavery. In his work during the Second

Great Awakening, he longed for the transformation of souls as well as the transformation of injustice. He viewed the work of God in this period of time to the work of God's grace.

> Some of the most open enemies have been bowed to sovereign grace, and brought to sit at the feet of Jesus, and in their right mind. We have, I believe, not but few prayer-less families among us in comparison to what there were previous to the awakening. Within about two months we have had about sixty who have made a profession of religion and joined the church; and a great number more will probably soon come forward. [The whole number added to the church was one hundred and three.] Thus it has pleased the Lord to do wonders among us, to the praise of his glorious grace.[50]

Haynes viewed God's activity during this time as a comprehensive, transformative work of grace.

Grace in the Abolition Movement

Richard Allen was a writer, pastor, educator, and leader who committed his life to helping people respond to the implications of the gospel. He wanted African-Americans to be afforded the same freedoms as whites in America. He also wanted whites to properly view blacks as equals. The deep hypocrisy in the church brought him great grief, not only slavery, but the unequal treatment of gospel ministers of African descent in the Methodist church.

Students of history might imagine Allen would become bitter and have deep unrighteous anger toward those who dismissed his arguments that God created all men equal. Even as he worked on missiological efforts, applying the implications of the gospel to make disciples, he always encouraged African-Americans in the spirit of grace:

> That God who knows the hearts of all men, and the propensity of a slave to hate his oppressor, hath strictly forbidden it to his chosen people, "Thou shalt not abhor an Egyptian, because thou wast a stranger in his land" (Deut. 23:7). The meek and humble Jesus, the great pattern of humanity, and every other virtue that can adorn and dignify men, hath commanded to love our enemies, to do good to them that hate and despitefully use us. I feel the obligations, I wish to impress them on the minds of our colored brethren, and that we may all forgive you, as we wish to be forgiven, we think it a great mercy to have all anger and bitterness removed from our minds; I appeal to your own feelings, if it is not very disquieting to feel yourselves under dominion of wrathful disposition.
>
> If you love your children, if you love your country, if you love the God of love, clear your hands from slaves, burthen not your children or your country with them, my heart has been sorry for the blood shed of the oppressors, as well as the oppressed, both appear guilty of each other's blood, in the sight of him who hath said, he that sheddeth man's blood, by man shall his blood be shed.[51]

His profound statement of reprieve is rooted in the person and work of Jesus Christ. Jesus' love, which Edwards would say flows from grace, was a staple in Allen's ministry, so much so that he pioneered starting one of the oldest African-American churches and denominations in the country. This led to the planting of many churches that would hold to Allen's Christ-centered vision.

Civil Rights Movement

Although the civil rights movement isn't solely a Christian movement, most of the greatest contributors are. If one takes a closer look at who and what motivated the movement's nonviolent philosophy, one will find Jesus and His sacrificial love at the center of what motivated them to see this issue Christianly.

Dr. Martin Luther King speaks from his own perspective about the roots of the civil rights movement and the love of Christ:

> I have tried to stand between these two forces, saying that we need emulate neither the "do nothingism" of the complacent nor the hatred and despair of the black nationalist. For there is the more excellent way of love and nonviolent protest. I am grateful to God that, through the influence of the Negro church, the way of nonviolence became an integral part of our struggle. If this philosophy had not emerged, by now many streets of the South would, I am convinced, be flowing with blood. And I am further convinced that if our white brothers dismiss as "rabble rousers" and "outside agitators" those of us who employ nonviolent direct action, and if they refuse to support our nonviolent efforts, millions of Negroes will, out of frustration and despair, seek solace and security in black nationalist ideologies—a development that would inevitably lead to a frightening racial nightmare.
>
> Was not Jesus an extremist for love: "Love your enemies, bless them that curse you, do good to them that

hate you, and pray for them which despitefully use you, and persecute you." Was not Amos an extremist for justice: "Let justice roll down like waters and righteousness like an ever flowing stream." Was not Paul an extremist for the Christian gospel: "I bear in my body the marks of the Lord Jesus." Was not Martin Luther an extremist: "Here I stand; I cannot do otherwise, so help me God." And John Bunyan: "I will stay in jail to the end of my days before I make a butchery of my conscience." Will we be extremists for hate or for love? . . . In that dramatic scene on Calvary's hill three men were crucified. We must never forget that all three were crucified for the same crime—the crime of extremism. Two were extremists for immorality, and thus fell below their environment. The other, Jesus Christ, was an extremist for love, truth and goodness, and thereby rose above his environment. Perhaps the South, the nation and the world are in dire need of creative extremists.[52]

For Dr. King, Jesus' life and death and the legacy of Christians in history who drew on the grace of God found strength to represent God's ideals because He gave them the power to do so. Grace is the key to experience the love of God. King saw that the grace of God through a display of restraint and radical commitment to confront evil would overcome ignorance.

Conclusion

As we can see, the Lord is deeply concerned with making sure that grace is kept on the agenda of the people of God. From the Jerusalem council to today, God is concerned for grace to be our relational foundation with Him. Grace should saturate our everyday experience with Him. The Lord recognizes that we are prone to operate outside of grace's influence, but like a Shepherd, He leaves the ninety-nine in pursuit of the one.

5

COMPLETING WORK
OF GRACE

It is interesting to know that the hymn "Amazing Grace" was not a popular hymn in Europe. It very well could have faded into obscurity. However, in the Southern part of the United States, "Amazing Grace" flourished, especially among slaves. Since Newton did not write it with a particular melody or song structure in mind, others fixed its musical arrangement at a later date. Some also added other stanzas—the last stanza that we sing today was not written by Newton, but added later and popularized by slaves. This eschatological (a vision of the coming kingdom of God) verse gives hope to all who sing it. Today, it is taken for granted as an integral part of the hymn, sung with hands raised in glorious worship for all Christians from every culture and ethnicity.

When we've been there ten thousand years,
Bright shining as the sun,
We've no less days to sing God's praise,
Than when we first begun.

As we live in this day and age, we find ourselves longing for the eternal when the fullness of God's grace will be dispensed to us. Yet, between now and eternity we are to look forward to this grace and pursue living in light of it.

Grace Will Lead Me Home

Jesus, in the close of John 1:35–51, talks to the disciples about the culmination of all things. He implies that their lives will be intricately connected to the events that will come to pass.

In verse 47, Jesus demonstrated supernatural insight into Nathaniel's life. He said Nathaniel was "an Israelite . . . in whom there is no deceit!" (ESV).

In other words, "What you see is what you get with you, Nate."

Another way of putting it is, "Nate, you keep it real," a.k.a. "you keep it 100," as we say in hood vernacular. It seems as if Jesus admires him for being a guy that is straight up with where he is and what he is feeling. Nathaniel, surprised, replied back, "How do you know me?"

Jesus answered, "Before Philip called you, when you were under the fig tree, I saw you" (v. 48). His answer rocked Nathaniel's world because now he understood that Jesus knew what was said about Him, as well as the skepticism that Nate had as he came to Jesus.

Quickly, Nathaniel affirms Phillip's statement about Jesus, "Rabbi, you are the Son of God! You are the King of Israel!" (v. 49). He is literally calling Jesus the explainer of all things (Rabbi), God (Son of God), and Lord (King of Israel). All of these titles are messianic in origin. These titles are a powerful fusion of the power and identity of Jesus Christ. It is doubtful whether Nathaniel understood the full meaning of his statement at this point. However, it is clear that he is submitting to the Lordship of Jesus.

All of the aforementioned titles point to the fact that Jesus fulfilled all of the promises concerning the Messiah in the Old Testament. Each title is both transcendent and imminent. There have been those in the Bible who were called by one or more of these three titles. For example, many other men in Jesus' day were called Rabbi. And in ancient Israel, kings were called Son of God and the king of Israel. However, Jesus is the truest teacher, the only legitimate Son of God, and king of all of Israel. Jesus is the only Rabbi who has intimately received His teaching through an eternal relationship with God the Father (John 1:18). As Son of God, Jesus is the only one who has a unique eternal relationship with the Father (in His deity) who is also embodied through the incarnation (in His humanity) as we see in John 5. And as King of Israel, Jesus is the one, true Davidic king (John 12:13).

With each one of these titles, these would-be disciples needed their basic understanding of how Jesus fulfilled each of these titles expanded through a grace-filled relationship with Him—under His divine Lordship—to gain perspective. We have the benefit of looking into this text with a greater understanding because of our position in history, but we still need Jesus to more deeply reveal Himself to us. That is the power of having a relationship with Him; we are able to come to a deeper knowledge of who He is and join Him in His redemptive efforts of earth.

You Ain't Seen Nothing Yet

Like the song by Bachman-Turner Overdrive, *"You ain't seen nothin yet, B-b-b-baby, you just ain't seen n-n-nothin' yet, Here's something that you never gonna forget, B-b-b-baby, you just ain't seen n-n-nothin' yet . . ."*

Jesus responded to him, "Do you believe only because I told you I saw you under the fig tree? You will see greater things than this" (John 1:50). First off, Jesus loves it when people simply believe Him based on His word. But He promises that He will not only show them what happened in the past, but also point them toward the good things He has in store for them in the future. Jesus promises that, in a relationship with Him, He'll affirm His identity over and over again. They will see greater things through the grace-filled experience of having Jesus continue to unveil all things.

Several times in my life I have enjoyed backstage passes to large events with well-known stars. Most people can gain access as a part of the general audience, but only a select few are given access to come into personal contact with the artists backstage. Anyone can buy a ticket to the show, but only those who are shown special favor by someone on the inside is able to get the backstage experience. Jesus just let these men know they will have both a front seat ticket and a backstage pass to experience Him.

Verse 51 further explains this reality. Jesus said, "I assure you: You will see heaven opened and the angels of God ascending and descending on the Son of Man." Jesus is pointing them back to Genesis 28:10–22, where Jacob leaves his homeland with his father for a different land. He sees a vision on the way: "And he dreamed: and behold, there was a ladder set up on the earth, and the top of it reached to heaven. And behold, the angels of God were ascending and descending on it!" (ESV). For Jacob, it was the Lord revealing to him that he will be with him and restore both his heritage and home. However, this dream has particular significance to Jesus and His ministry. Jesus states that He is the ladder that Jacob saw with the Lord standing at the top. Jesus pledges that He is going to reopen heaven to man again. He would be the way in which all things would be restored back to God. Jesus would be the one to reconnect heaven to earth, God to man.

Here, as elsewhere in this first chapter, we have a vague reference to that which will become clear in what follows: in this case, the fact that Jesus fulfills and thus replaces the revelation to Israel (cf. 1:17–18). He is in truth greater than Jacob (Jn 4:12), for he is the real Jacob-Israel, the locus and source of the real people of God (cf. Dodd 1953:244–46; Kim 1985:82–86). It also means that "Jesus as Son of Man has become the locus of divine glory, the point of contact between heaven and earth. The disciples are promised figuratively that they will come to see this; and indeed, at Cana they do see his glory" (Brown 1966:91). Jacob's exclamation that "This is none other than the house of God; this is the gate of heaven" (Gen 28:17) is fulfilled in Jesus, who is himself the temple (Jn 2:19–21) and the gate (Jn 10:7). But there is no literal vision of angels later in the story such as is mentioned in this verse. Rather, this verse is the clue to the significance of everything that follows in the Gospel (Dodd 1953:294). Specifically, the promise here is that they will recognize who Jesus really is and thereby see God, for John uses the term *Son of Man* to speak of Jesus' deity manifested in humanity (cf. comments on 3:13–14; 5:27). This promise is fulfilled when Thomas sees the crucified one now living and confesses, "My Lord and my God!" (Jn 20:28). "Jesus

Christ *even in his humanity* is united to heaven and enjoys
perfect communion with God his Father." (Michaels
1989:43)[53]

Ultimately, Jesus will lead us home to God. Jesus came to forge
together heaven and earth. While He has a deep understanding of
heaven, He is able to empathize with the infirmities of earth (Heb.
4:15). The grace of God in Jesus Christ can be found in how Jesus
helps those on earth more effectively understand the kingdom of
heaven. As a disciple of Jesus Christ, our walk must reflect a commitment to deeply understand heaven and apply it fervently here
on earth. As Jesus said in the Lord's Prayer, "Thy will be done, on
earth as it is in heaven."

To see heaven opened, as it says in verse 51, isn't merely a heavenly vision or dream per se (although Peter does in Acts), but seeing
what was closed to man reopened to him. *See heaven opened.* This
is powerful! Jesus' ministry was and is a kingdom ministry. The
coming of the kingdom through Jesus Christ is seeing heaven open.
That is why He is called the key of David; that is why all of God's
promises find their "yes" and "amen" in Him. Jesus, when He was
casting out demons, turning water into wine, feeding the 5,000,
opening the eyes of the blind, preaching the gospel, ultimately
dying on the cross, and being raised from the grave is heaven opening. Heaven has been opened, but there is no need for us to ascend
because the Son of Man has come down to us. The one Isaiah saw
(Isa. 6:1–5; John 12:38–41) has come into our midst! Jesus, not
heaven, is the focal point of revelation.[54]

Already, but Not Yet?

When we get in the car, my children always ask my wife and me the same two questions all children ask, "Where are we going?" and "Are we there yet?" No matter how many times you tell them to be patient, they keep asking these questions. They are impatient with us getting them to the place we promised they'd go. But we struggle in the same way.

Like young children on a road trip, the disciples asked these same questions of Jesus. Over and over again in Jesus' ministry, He challenged the disciples with the fact that some things would be fulfilled now, and others later. The theme *already but not yet* runs throughout the Gospels. It is a tension that ties heaven to earth—the in-breaking of the kingdom.

Jesus has fulfilled all things, but not all has been fully realized yet. In the mind of God, we who are in Christ are fully perfected in Him (Rom. 8:29–30), but He is still dealing with mess in our lives. One day we will be fully perfected (2 Cor. 5:1–10), but until then we are to work out our own salvation with fear and trembling (Phil. 2:12). There will be times in which God will heal people (Matt. 8:14–17; James 5:14–18), and then there will be times where He doesn't (2 Cor. 12:1–10). Both occasions are under His Lordship and under His grace. To think that God will solve everything in this life is to have our eyes closed to heaven; to think that God won't change anything in this life is to have our eyes closed to heaven. Living in the tension of the *already but not yet* is to live in fervent submission to the sovereignty of God as He shows us the multifaceted nature of His grace. We mustn't shrink back from praying fervently, nor should we fall into a place of spiritual complacency where we expect nothing from God. Jesus seems to call us on a voyage with Him that calls us to see greater things.

These greater things must be seen from His perspective and not our own. Jesus tells the disciples that the greatest among them would be servants. We see over and over again that those who followed Jesus viewed greatness—among other things—differently than Jesus did. In our journey under the Lordship of Christ, we are forever having our view of greatness challenged by Him. The beautiful part of it is that we learn about it in an environment of grace.

At my high school, there was a new student who was about 5'5" and of a small poundage. He was pretty stocky, but really small. We were all more than a little shocked when he joined the wrestling team. We all looked at one another and thought, *What can this guy do?*

But once we started our workout, he outran us. When we started lifting, he out-lifted us. And when we wrestled him, he more than out-wrestled us. Later we found out that this guy was an All-American wrestling champion who was undefeated. When we looked at him, we assumed a lack of greatness. Likewise, Jesus tends to show the greatness of His grace in the most unlikely places. As disciples of Jesus, when we learn to stop fixing our eyes on what or whom He uses, we begin to see Him more clearly.

Extending the Boundaries of Grace

Many times it is not hard for us to see our need for the grace of God in our own lives, but the ongoing issue we all have to wrestle with is whether or not we will see the need for grace in the lives of others. But it's not enough to merely see deficits of grace; we must extend it to others as they break our hearts. In the midst of our punctures, pains, and perplexities, can we find the strength and courage to apply the grace of God toward them? Listen to Jerry Bridges's call to extend the boundaries of grace:

> Having experienced God's grace, we are then called on to extend that grace to others. The evidence of whether we are living by His grace is to be found in the way we treat other people. If we see ourselves as sinner and totally unworthy of God's compassion, patience, and forgiveness, then we will want to be gracious to others. . . . God's grace is indeed meant to be a transforming grace.[55]

As a pastor, it is daunting at times in dealing with brokenness on the front lines of ministry. Seeing so much brokenness and despair can be overwhelming.

I remember one of my mentors asking me, "Eric do you have hope?"

I looked at him like, "What do you mean do I have hope? Yes, I have hope."

I was offended at the question. He explained more clearly, "I'm not asking about hope for you, but hope for where God has sent you."

He went on to say, "You need more than just hope for you, but for where you are going."

I got the picture at that point. I needed hope that would cause me to extend the boundaries of God's grace. Jesus desires that, until He returns, we extend grace's borders through the power of the gospel. Greater works Jesus desires that, until He returns, we extend grace's borders through the power of the gospel. The extension of these borders is realized by heaven opening our eyes through how the gospel of grace can change issues in the uncharted areas of man's life.

Not long ago, a recovering addict became a part of our community. She was in and out of the church. We helped her, poured into her, and walked with her. There didn't seem to be much change. After another stretch in rehab, she came back to the ministry. Several of us were not as hopeful about the long-term effects of our ministry, nor rehab to her life. One Sunday after I preached, she came forward to profess her faith. The next week she was baptized. Now she is joining the church through membership and desires discipleship in her walk as a single mom. God is still at work in her, but she is teaching us about having eyes opened by heaven. It is wonderful to see God's grace unfold in someone else's life.

CONCLUSION

BEAT GOD TO THE PUNCH

If anyone hears My words and doesn't keep them,
I do not judge him; for I did not come to judge
the world but to save the world.

—JOHN 12:47

Jesus Christ came to empower us to *beat God to the punch*. Beating God to the punch was God's idea; we are not fooling Him or anyone else. God's idea in eternity past was to provide Jesus as a substitution for our sin. There is a Judge and judgment coming.

Two Types of Freedom

Every time I share my faith with someone, I am bewildered when someone doesn't place his or her trust in Jesus. How could someone turn down something so valuable that is offered so freely? People say that nothing in this life is free. That may be true when it comes to economics, but it's not the case when it comes to grace.

Because of the price that Jesus paid on your behalf, a relationship with God is offered completely free of charge.

Not all view God's offer with excitement. Some seem to think that you have to do something meritorious to be accepted by God. Jesus asked the religious establishment,

> "For which is easier: to say, 'Your sins are forgiven,' or to say, 'Get up and walk'? But so you may know that the Son of Man has authority on earth to forgive sins"—then He told the paralytic, "Get up, pick up your mat, and go home." (Matt. 9:5–6)

Jesus wanted them to know the offer of forgiveness that was offered through His life. His miracles were always to point to who He is and by whose authority He made such radical claims. Jesus has the authority to offer the forgiveness of sins. Yet, sometimes, even forgiven people still wrestle with the radically free nature of forgiveness.

In Acts 15, some of the believers that came to Jerusalem had a rough time accepting that non-Jewish believers who trusted Christ were secure in salvation. They wanted to add requirements to the gospel. They said, "Unless you are circumcised according to the custom prescribed by Moses, you cannot be saved!" (15:1). Though they had been forgiven, they struggled with the extending borders of grace. But no one can control the commitment of Jesus to save sinners.

Even today, people try to add to the gospel. Whether it is judging someone's ethics, their political party, their denomination, or their theology, we use things that are intended for good as weapons against one another. We must keep the gospel uncluttered from our own preferences. We don't have to save the gospel from other people; it is to be offered freely. The gospel doesn't need rescuing; we do.

The Holy Spirit is the one who affirms and strengthens a person for conversion. No one can confess Jesus as Lord without the Spirit of God (1 Cor. 12:3). Therefore, He is a better monitor of someone's transformation than we are. Our job is simple: to preach the gospel and make disciples. One of the greatest comforts to me in the gospel is that God does the saving, not me. Redemption is such a great and powerful work that we don't have to work at all.

Freedom of Experience

One of my favorite verses on freedom is Galatians 5:1, "For freedom Christ has set us free; stand firm therefore, and do not submit again to a yoke of slavery" (ESV). The purpose statement in the beginning of the verse says it all, *For freedom* . . . our purpose in being freed by God is to be taken out of bondage to live the life we were meant to live for His glory. Beating God to the punch is marked by coming in contact daily with the freedom that comes through Jesus' finished work on the cross. Jesus offers real freedom. All other human talk of freedom is cloaked bondage.

There is no freedom unless we are experiencing life on God's terms. But most see God's freedom through Christ as bondage. A popular anecdote about an elephant fits here:

> As a man was passing the elephants, he suddenly stopped, confused by the fact that these huge creatures were being held by only a small rope tied to their front leg. No chains, no cages. It was obvious that the elephants

could, at anytime, break away from their bonds but for some reason, they did not. He saw a trainer nearby and asked why these animals just stood there and made no attempt to get away. "Well," trainer said, "when they are very young and much smaller we use the same size rope to tie them and, at that age, it's enough to hold them. As they grow up, they are conditioned to believe they cannot break away. They believe the rope can still hold them, so they never try to break free."

The man was amazed. These animals could at any time break free from their bonds but because they believed they couldn't, they were stuck right where they were.[56]

This is what the world does to us. From birth, sin trains us to think we are truly free, though we are really still in bondage. But in Jesus Christ, we *are* truly free! Jesus states it the best in John 8:36, "So if the Son sets you free, you will be free indeed" (ESV). In other words, we are free *for real for real*.

The Coming Judgment, and the Grace-Filled Path to Deliverance

Comparatively, there is another side to this. Those who don't know Jesus Christ as their substitution for sin live under the wrath of God. To live under the wrath of God is to be held personally accountable for one's sins. Because God is holy, He expects and holds humans accountable to be holy as He is holy. God is not only saving people by faith in Christ from sin, Satan, self, and the world—but also His wrath (Rom. 5:9). God's wrath is His justified anger against the sinfulness of man. Psalm 5:5 says, "The boastful cannot stand in Your presence; You *hate* all evildoers" (emphasis mine).

Someone would say, "Isn't God contradicting Himself? How can he be a God who hates and loves?" But God is the only one who has the right to hate. He isn't negatively affected by it; His hate is related to His expectation that all live for the purpose He created them.

Someone else might say, "Even the Bible seems to have two Gods in it: the hateful and cruel God of the Old Testament, and the loving, compassionate God of the New Testament." But God is the same yesterday, today, and forever. God shows love toward us by being patient in not destroying those who have sinned against Him—though our sins certainly merit it. God doesn't demand justice for our sin immediately (2 Pet. 3:9). That is love! He also demonstrates His love for us in that while in our sinful state, He sent Jesus to die in our place (Rom. 5:8; 10:5–21). Rather than giving sinners the cup of wrath we all have earned in our trespasses, Jesus drank it on our behalf.

Jesus will judge all who are not under His banner:

> When the Lord Jesus is revealed from heaven with his mighty angels in flaming fire, inflicting vengeance on those who do not know God and on those who do not obey the gospel of our Lord Jesus. (2 Thess. 1:7–8 ESV)

In both testaments of the Bible God is displayed as both loving and wrathful. In the Old Testament we see His wrath poured out through the flood (Gen. 6–7). Later the same Noah who built the ark gets punch drunk, but the Lord doesn't deal with him according to his sin (Gen. 9:21). Later we see David commit adultery, murder, and tries to bear false witness, both of which two are worthy of death, and the Lord forgives and cleanses him of his sin

(2 Sam. 12:13). Meanwhile in the New Testament, we see Jesus proclaim the expansive love of God in John 3, yet the same God kills Ananias and Sapphira for lying on their giving statements. The purpose of God's wrath is not to destroy mankind (Hos. 11:9). Neither is it vindictive, emotional, overreactive, or out of control. Even in His wrath, He sovereignly imposes limits on nations (Babylon, Assyria) and disciplines His own people with the desired end that they return to Him (Joel 2:13–14). The eschatological expectation of the Old Testament concept of the Day of the Lord includes the restoration of the earth, when the whole earth will be filled with the knowledge (Isa. 11:9; Hab. 2:14) and glory (Nah. 14:21; Ps. 72:19) of the Lord and wickedness will be no more (Isa. 65:25).[57] God's wrath and discipline is never divorced from His mercy and grace.

Hell Is for Real

To make it plain, hell is the full unveiling of the wrath of God. Hell is eternal torment to pay for one's sin. It is God giving man what He deserves by delivering man over to live under His wrath forever. Because forever is what it will take for man to pay for his sins, 2 Peter 2:4–6 shows clearly that hell is the place of God's wrath. God is coming back to judge us through Jesus Christ and is going to ultimately make those who did not place their faith in Jesus spend eternity separated from His grace, mercy, and love, but they will live in His wrath against their sin forever and ever (Rev. 20:13–14). One scholar describes hell this way:

> Hell is the final destiny of unbelievers and is variously
> described by the figures of a furnace of fire, eternal fire,

eternal punishment (Mt 13:42, 50; 25:41, 46); outer darkness, the place of weeping and torment (8:12); eternal sin
(Mk 3:29); the wrath of God (Rom 2:5); everlasting sepa-
ration from the Lord, never to see the glory of his power
(2 Thes 1:9); the bottomless pit (Rv 9:1, 11); continuous
torment (14:10, 11); the lake of fire, the second death
(21:8); a place for the devil and his demons (Mt 25:41).
The foregoing designations clearly show that the state of
those in hell is one of eternal duration.[58]

Once the eternal wrath of God is revealed to men, those who
don't know Jesus will not have a chance to believe in Him after the
clock runs out. It will be over. Because of that, why not beat God
to the punch?

Thank God for Jesus Christ

In order to beat God to the punch, you have to place your
trust in Jesus Christ. Jesus states it plainly in John 3:18, "Anyone
who believes in Him is not condemned, but anyone who does not
believe is already condemned, because he has not believed in the
name of the One and Only Son of God." It is the first step toward
a grace-filled life.

Jesus, on the cross, took God's best shot. He took on the fullness of God's hatred toward sin (2 Cor. 5:21). Jesus wasn't guilty for
our sin, but had our guilt placed upon Him and was treated like
the guiltiest of sinners, in order that our guilt would be removed
through faith.

Jesus was wounded for our transgressions and bruised for our
iniquity, the chastisement of our peace was upon Him, and by His
stripes we were healed. In other words, He took our beat down. Jesus

died under the full blast of God's wrath and remained faithful. Three days later He got up out of the grave with all power in His hands.

For the Believer

Life and life more abundantly is what He gives us who believe. If you know Jesus Christ as your Lord and Savior, you should be committed to living this grace-filled life. For those of us who understand on some level and know that God's wrath has been removed from hovering over us, we should be passionately pursuing and experiencing all of the benefits that grace affords us. The grace-filled life will turn into the grace-filled eternity:

> Then I saw a new heaven and a new earth, for the first heaven and the first earth had passed away, and the sea no longer existed. I also saw the Holy City, new Jerusalem, coming down out of heaven from God, prepared like a bride adorned for her husband. Then I heard a loud voice from the throne: Look! God's dwelling is with humanity, and He will live with them. They will be His people, and God Himself will be with them and be their God. He will wipe away every tear from their eyes. Death will no longer exist; grief, crying, and pain will exist no longer, because the previous things have passed away.
>
> Then the One seated on the throne said, "Look! I am making everything new." He also said, "Write, because these words are faithful and true." And He said to me, "It is done! I am the Alpha and the Omega, the Beginning and the End. I will give water as a gift to the thirsty from the spring of life. The victor will inherit these things, and I will be his God, and he will be My son. (Rev. 21:1–7)

APPENDIX

SUMMARY TABLE[59]

Figure	Period	The Grace Given	What Grace Does	What Grace Motivates
Basil of Caesarea	ca. 329–379	The Holy Spirit and grace at baptism	Makes believers children of God	Living a new life in Christ and being conformed to His image
Athanasius of Alexandria	ca. 296–373	-	Allows believers to become like God	-
John Chrysostom	ca. 347–407	Righteousness and sanctification	Makes believers sons of God	Enables holy living
Augustine	ca. 354–430	The gift of grace in Jesus Christ	Overcomes original sin and enables living a godly life	Continued perseverance

Martin Luther	1483–1546	Christ's righteousness in justification	Places believers in right standing before God	Peace before God and the means for holy living
John Calvin	1509–1564	Reconciliation and sanctification through union with Christ	Makes believers blameless before God	The cultivation of a holy life
Jonathan Edwards	1703–1758	The Holy Spirit in salvation	Gives believers new life in Christ	Love for the things of the Spirit
George Whitefield	1714–1770	Being elect in Christ	Enables belief in Christ	-
Henry Ward Beecher	1813–1887	Forgiveness	Given unconditionally but received upon repentance	-
Charles Finney	1792–1875	Holy Spirit	Persuades people to act rightly	Enables moral behavior
Lemuel Haynes	1753–1833	Salvation	Opens eyes to receive forgiveness	-
Richard Allen	1760–1831	Forgiveness and redemption	Makes forgiveness possible	Motivates love without seeking revenge
Frederick Douglass	1818–1895	Opportunity to love others	Kept him free from harm	-

NOTES

1. W. A. Elwell, *Baker Encyclopedia of the Bible* (Grand Rapids: Baker, 1988).

2. M. G. Easton, *Easton's Bible Dictionary* (Oak Harbor, WA: Logos Research Systems, Inc., 1996), c1897.

3. Ibid.

4. L. Morris, *The Gospel According to John,* The New International Commentary on the New Testament (Grand Rapids: Eerdmans, 1995), 137.

5. Ibid.

6. Aspect: "Snapshot: The aorist tense presents an occurrence in summary, viewed as a whole from the outside, without regard for the internal make-up of the occurrence." Daniel Wallace, *Greek Grammar Beyond the Basics,* 555.

7. Andreas J. Köstenberger, *John, Baker Exegetical Commentary on the New Testament* (Grand Rapids: Baker Academic, 2004), 73.

8. It is worth noting that "follow" is not used in the rest of the NT. Further references in John are found in 1:38, 40, 43; 8:12; 10:4, 5, 27; 12:26; 13:36–37; 21:19, 22. Also see Köstenberger 1998b: 145–47, 177–80.

9. For further rabbinic parallels, see Köstenberger 1998a: 119.

10. Köstenberger, *John, Baker Exegetical Commentary on the New Testament,* 73. See the discussions in Morris 1995: 137; R. Brown 1966: 78; Carson 1991: 154; Barrett 1978: 180. See also comments on the term μένω (*menō*, stay) at 1:39.

11. D. A. Carson, *The Gospel According to John* (Grand Rapids: Eerdmans, 1991), 154.

12. See http://www.followtherabbi.com/journey/israel/to-be-a-talmid1.

13. A. C. Myers, *The Eerdmans Bible Dictionary* (Grand Rapids: Eerdmans, 1987).

14. Note that these are the first words of Jesus in John's gospel. Witherington (1995: 69) notes that in dramatic works the first words of the main character are often of special importance (more doubtful is Witherington's association of Jesus with Wisdom beckoning for an audience [pp. 69–70]). Whitacre (1999: 71) observes John's emphasis on Jesus' "almost mysterious silence" in comparison with the other Gospels, where "Jesus teaches, preaches and calls people to follow him, yet here Jesus has said almost nothing. . . . Compared with the Synoptics' picture, Jesus in John appears as one hidden and aloof." However, this comment surely must be balanced by the theme of Jesus' humanity in John's Gospel (see, e.g., Jesus' weariness from travel in John 4 or his bursting into tears in John 11).

15. Köstenberger, *John, Baker Exegetical Commentary on the New Testament*, 74.

16. Craig S. Keener, *The IVP Bible Background Commentary: New Testament* (Downers Grove, IL: InterVarsity Press, 1993), S. Jn 1:38.

17. The process by which we grow from spiritual infancy to spiritual maturity.

18. Jonathan Edwards, *A Treatise Concerning Religious Affections: In Three Parts* (Oak Harbor, WA: Logos Research Systems, Inc., 1996).

19. C. E. Arnold, *Zondervan Illustrated Bible Backgrounds Commentary: John, Acts,* Vol. 2 (Grand Rapids: Zondervan, 2002), 19.

20. D. A. Carson, *The Gospel According to John*, 156.

21. See Cullmann, *TDNT* 6:100–101; Borchert 1996: 143–44; Burge 2000: 76; Morris 1995: 140.

22. Cf. Matt. 16:16–19; see Schnackenburg 1990: 1.312–13; R. Brown 1966: 80; Beasley-Murray 1987: 27; Carson 1984: 368. It must be noted, however, that the Evangelist himself does not comment explicitly, apparently leaving it up to the reader to draw the proper inference (see Barrett 1978: 183).

23. Köstenberger, *John, Baker Exegetical Commentary on the New Testament*, 77–78.

24. Eugene H. Peterson, *A Long Obedience in the Same Direction: Discipleship in an Instant Society* (Kindle Locations 103–104), Kindle Edition.

25. *The NET Bible First Edition* (Biblical Studies Press, 2006), John 1:29, notes.

26. W. A. Elwell, *Baker Encyclopedia of the Bible* (Grand Rapids: Baker, 1988), 1300.

27. W. D. J. Tucker in D. N. Freedman, A. C. Myers, and A. B. Beck, Eds., *Eerdmans Dictionary of the Bible* (Grand Rapids: Eerdmans, 2000), Rabbi, Rabboni, 1106.

28. J. Swanson, and O. Nave, *New Nave's Topical Bible* (Oak Harbor, WA: Logos Research Systems, 1994).

> Adam, 1 Cor. 15:45. Advocate, 1 John 2:1. Almighty, Rev. 1:8. Alpha and Omega, Rev. 1:8. Amen, Rev. 3:14. Angel, Gen. 48:16; Ex. 23:20, 21. Angel of his presence, Isa. 63:9. Anointed, Ps. 2:2. Apostle, Heb. 3:1. Arm of the Lord, Isa. 51:9, 10. Author and perfecter of our faith, Heb. 12:2. Beginning and end of the creation of God, Rev. 3:14; 22:13. Beloved, Eph. 1:6. Bishop, 1 Pet. 2:25. Blessed and only Potentate, 1 Tim. 6:15. Branch, Jer. 23:5; Zech. 3:8. Bread of life, John 6:48. Bridegroom, Matt. 9:15. Bright and morning star, Rev. 22:16. Brightness of the Father's glory, Heb. 1:3. Captain of the Lord's army, Josh. 5:14. Captain of salvation, Heb. 2:10. Carpenter, Mark 6:3. Carpenter's son, Matt. 13:55. Chief Shepherd, 1 Pet. 5:4. Chief corner stone, 1 Pet. 2:6. Outstanding among ten thousand, Song 5:10. Child, Isa. 9:6; Luke 2:27, 43. Chosen of God, 1 Pet. 2:4. Christ, Matt. 1:16; Luke 9:20. The Christ, Matt. 16:20; Mark 14:61. Christ, a King, Luke 23:2. Christ Jesus, Acts 19:4; Rom. 3:24; 8:1; 1 Cor. 1:2; 1 Cor. 1:30; Heb. 3:1; 1 Pet. 5:10, 14. Christ Jesus our Lord, 1 Tim. 1:12; Rom. 8:39. Christ of God, Luke 9:20. Christ, the chosen of God, Luke 23:35. Christ the Lord, Luke 2:11; Christ the power of God, 1 Cor. 1:24. Christ the wisdom of God, 1 Cor. 1:24. Christ, the Son of God, Acts 9:20. Christ, Son of the Blessed, Mark 14:61. Commander, Isa. 55:4. Consolation of Israel, Luke 2:25. Corner stone, Eph. 2:20. Counselor, Isa. 9:6. Covenant of the people, Isa. 42:6. David, Jer. 30:9. Daysman, Job 9:33.

Dayspring, Luke 1:78. Day star, 2 Pet. 1:19. Deliverer, Rom. 11:26. Desire of all nations, Hag. 2:7. Door, John 10:7. Elect, Isa. 42:1. Emmanuel, Isa. 7:14. Ensign, Isa. 11:10. Eternal life, 1 John 5:20. Everlasting Father, Isa. 9:6. Faithful and True, Rev. 19:11. Faithful witness, Rev. 1:5. Faithful and true witness, Rev. 3:14. Finisher of faith, Heb. 12:2. First and last, Rev. 1:17; 2:8; 22:13. First begotten, Heb. 1:6. First begotten of the dead, Rev. 1:5. Firstborn, Ps. 89:27. Foundation, Isa. 28:16. Fountain, Zech. 13:1. Forerunner, Heb. 6:20. Friend of sinners, Matt. 11:19. Gift of God, John 4:10. Glory of Israel, Luke 2:32. God, John 1:1. God blessed for ever, Rom. 9:5. God manifest in the flesh, 1 Tim. 3:16. God of Israel, the Savior, Isa. 45:15. God of the whole earth, Isa. 54:5. God our Savior, 1 Tim. 2:3. God's dear Son, Col. 1:13. God with us, Matt. 1:23. Good Master, Matt. 19:16. Governor, Matt. 2:6. Great shepherd of the sheep, Heb. 13:20. Head of the church, Eph. 5:23. Heir of all things, Heb. 1:2. High priest, Heb. 4:14. Head of every man, 1 Cor. 11:3. Head of the church, Col. 1:18. Head of the corner, Matt. 21:42. Holy child Jesus, Acts 4:30. Holy one, Ps. 16:10; Acts 3:14. Holy one of God, Mark 1:24. Holy one of Israel, Isa. 41:14; 54:5. Holy thing, Luke 1:35. Hope [our], 1 Tim. 1:1. Horn of salvation, Luke 1:69. I Am, John 8:58. Image of God, Heb. 1:3. Israel, Isa. 49:3. Jehovah, Isa. 40:3. Jehovah's fellow, Zech. 13:7. Jesus, Matt. 1:21. Jesus Christ, Matt. 1:1; John 1:17; 17:3; Acts 2:38; 4:10; 9:34; 10:36; 16:18; Rom. 1:1, 3, 6; 2:16; 5:15, 17; 6:3; 1 Cor. 1:1, 4; 1 Cor. 2:2; 2 Cor. 1:19; 4:6; 13:5; Gal. 2:16; Phil. 1:8; 2:11; 1 Tim. 1:15; Heb. 13:8; 1 John 1:7; 2:1. Jesus Christ our Lord, Rom. 1:3; 6:11, 23; 1 Cor. 1:9; 7:25. Jesus Christ our Savior, Titus 3:6. Jesus of Nazareth, Mark 1:24; Luke 24:19. Jesus of Nazareth, King of the Jews, John 19:19. Jesus, the King of the Jews, Matt. 27:37. Jesus, the Son of God, Heb. 4:14. Jesus, the Son of Joseph, John 6:42. Judge, Acts 10:42. Just man, Matt. 27:19. Just one, Acts 3:14; 7:52; 22:14. Just person, Matt. 27:24. King, Matt. 21:5. King of Israel, John 1:49. King of the Jews, Matt. 2:2. King of saints,

Rev. 15:3. King of kings, 1 Tim. 6:15; Rev. 17:14. King of glory, Ps. 24:7–10. King of Zion, Matt. 21:5. King over all the earth, Zech. 14:9. Lamb, Rev. 5:6, 8; 6:16; 7:9, 10, 17; 12:11; 13:8, 11; 14:1, 4; 15:3; 17:14; 19:7, 9; 21:9, 14, 22, 23, 27. Lamb of God, John 1:29. Lawgiver, Isa. 33:22. Leader, Isa. 55:4. Life, John 14:6. Light, John 8:12. Light, everlasting, Isa. 60:20. Light of the world, John 8:12. Light to the Gentiles, Isa. 42:6. Light, true, John 1:9. Living bread, John 6:51. Living stone, 1 Pet. 2:4. Lion of the tribe of Judah, Rev. 5:5. Lord, Rom. 1:3. Lord of lords, Rev. 17:14; 19:16. Lord of all, Acts 10:36. Lord our righteousness, Jer. 23:6. Lord God Almighty, Rev. 15:3. Lord from heaven, 1 Cor. 15:47. Lord and Savior Jesus Christ, 2 Pet. 1:11; 3:18. Lord Christ, Col. 3:24. Lord Jesus, Acts 7:59; Col. 3:17; 1 Thess. 4:2. Lord Jesus Christ, Acts 11:17; 16:31; 20:21; Rom. 5:1, 11; 13:14. Lord Jesus Christ our Savior, Titus 1:4. Lord of glory, Jas. 2:1. Lord of Armies, Isa. 44:6. Lord, mighty in battle, Psa. 24:8. Lord of the dead and living, Rom. 14:9. Lord of the sabbath, Mark 2:28. Lord over all, Rom. 10:12. Lord's Christ, Luke 2:26. Lord, strong and mighty, Ps. 24:8. Lord, the, our righteousness, Jer. 23:6. Lord, your holy one, Isa. 43:15. Lord, your redeemer, Isa. 43:14. Man Christ Jesus, 1 Tim. 2:5. One of sorrows, Isa. 53:3. Master, Matt. 23:8. Mediator, 1 Tim. 2:5. Messenger of the covenant, Mal. 3:1. Messiah, John 1:41. Messiah the Prince, Dan. 9:25. Mighty God, Isa. 9:6. Mighty one of Israel, Isa. 30:29. Mighty one of Jacob, Isa. 49:26. Mighty to save, Isa. 63:1. Minister of the sanctuary, Heb. 8:2. Morning star, Rev. 22:16. Most holy, Dan. 9:24. Most mighty, Ps. 45:3. Nazarene, Matt. 2:23. Offspring of David, Rev. 22:16. Only begotten, John 1:14. Only begotten of the Father, John 1:14. Only begotten son, John 1:18. Only wise God, our Savior, Jude 25. Passover, 1 Cor. 5:7. Plant of renown, Ezek. 34:29. Potentate, 1 Tim. 6:15. Power of God, 1 Cor. 1:24. Physician, Matt. 9:12. Precious corner stone, Isa. 28:16. Priest, Heb. 7:17. Prince, Acts 5:31. Prince of life, Acts 3:15. Prince of peace, Isa. 9:6. Prince of the kings of the earth, Rev. 1:5. Prophet,

Deut. 18:15, 18; Matt. 21:11; Luke 24:19. Propitiation, 1 John 2:2. Rabbi, John 1:49. Rabboni, John 20:16. Ransom, 1 Tim. 2:6. Redeemer, Isa. 59:20. Resurrection and life, John 11:25. Redemption, 1 Cor. 1:30. Righteous branch, Jer. 23:5. Righteous judge, 2 Tim. 4:8. Righteous servant, Isa. 53:11. Righteousness, 1 Cor. 1:30. Rock, 1 Cor. 10:4. Rock of offence, 1 Pet. 2:8. Root of David, Rev. 5:5; 22:16. Root of Jesse, Isa. 11:10. Rose of Sharon, Song 2:1. Ruler in Israel, Mic. 5:2. Salvation, Luke 2:30. Sanctification, 1 Cor. 1:30. Sanctuary, Isa. 8:14. Savior, Luke 2:11. Savior, Jesus Christ, 2 Tim. 1:10; Titus 2:13; 2 Pet. 1:1. Savior of the body, Eph. 5:23. Savior of the world, 1 John 4:14. Scepter, Num. 24:17. Second Adam, 1 Cor. 15:47. Seed of David, 2 Tim. 2:8. Seed of the woman, Gen. 3:15. Servant, Isa. 42:1. Servant of rulers, Isa. 49:7. Shepherd, Mark 14:27. Shepherd and bishop of souls, 1 Pet. 2:25. Shepherd, chief, 1 Pet. 5:4. Shepherd, good, John 10:11. Shepherd, great, Heb. 13:20. Shepherd of Israel, Ps. 80:1. Shiloh, Gen. 49:10. Son of the Father, 2 John 3. Son of God, see Son of God. Son of Man, see Son of Man. Son of the blessed, Mark 14:61. Son of the highest, Luke 1:32. Son of David, Matt. 9:27. Star, Num. 24:17. Sun of righteousness, Mal. 4:2. Surety, Heb. 7:22. Stone, Matt. 21:42. Stone of stumbling, 1 Pet. 2:8. Sure foundation, Isa. 28:16. Teacher, John 3:2. True God, 1 John 5:20. True vine, John 15:1. Truth, John 14:6. Unspeakable gift, 2 Cor. 9:15. Very Christ, Acts 9:22. Vine, John 15:1. Way, John 14:6. Which is, which was, which is to come, Rev. 1:4. Wisdom, Prov. 8:12. Wisdom of God, 1 Cor. 1:24. Witness, Isa. 55:4; Rev. 1:5. Wonderful, Isa. 9:6. Word, John 1:1. Word of God, Rev. 19:13. Word of life, 1 John 1:1. Those who use his name must depart from evil, 2 Tim. 2:19.

29. Fredrick M. Lehman, "The Love of God," 1919.

30. P. Ellingworth, *The Epistle to the Hebrews: A Commentary on the Greek Text* (Grand Rapids: Eerdmans, 1993), 541.

31. R. C. Stedman, *Hebrews* (Downers Grove, IL: InterVarsity Press, 1992), Heb. 10:26.

32. Some have suggested that *the Spirit of grace* may be an allusion to or echo of Zech. 12:10 LXX, where God promised to pour forth upon the house of David "a spirit of grace and mercy." Lane, 2:294, thinks that, if this is intended, the reference is to the Holy Spirit "poured out" at Pentecost, "who offers himself to the community in free grace and effects salvation" (Michel, 353).

33. On this view the genitive τῆς χάριτος ("of grace") is adjectival; Ellingworth, 541; note BDAG, 1080.

34. D. A. Carson, *The Letter to the Hebrews* (Grand Rapids: Eerdmans, 2010), 379.

35. L. Koehler, W. Baumgartner, M. E. J. Richardson, and J. J. Stamm, *The Hebrew and Aramaic Lexicon of the Old Testament* (Leiden; New York: E. J. Brill, 1999), "*hesed.*"

36. J. Swanson, *Dictionary of Biblical Languages with Semantic Domains: Hebrew (Old Testament)* (Oak Harbor, WA: Logos Research Systems, Inc., 1997), "*hesed.*"

37. Sinclair B. Ferguson, *By Grace Alone: How the Grace of God Amazes Me* (Lake Mary, FL: Reformation Trust Pub., 2010), 66.

38. Martin Luther, *The Bondage of the Will,* trans. J. I. Packer and O. R. Johnston (Grand Rapids: Revell, 1990, reprint), 44.

39. Caesar A. W. Clark, "Christ the Center of History," *Outstanding Black Sermons* Vol. 2, Walter B. Hoard, ed. (Valley Forge: Judson Press, 1979), 29.

40. Ibid., 21.

41. See Eugene TeSelle, "Pelagius, Pelagianism," *Augustine through the Ages,* ed. Allan D. Fitzgerald (Grand Rapids: Eerdmans, 1999), 633–40.

42. Martin Luther, "Preface to Romans," trans. Andrew Thornton, http://www.ccel.org/l/luther/romans/pref_romans.html.

43. John Calvin, *Institutes of the Christian Religion, 1559,* ed. J. T. McNeill and F. L. Battles (Philadelphia, PA: Westminster Press, 1960), 3.11.1, 725.

44. J. Todd Billings, "Milbank's Theology of 'The Gift,' and Calvin's Theology of Grace: A Critical Comparison," *Modern Theology* 21, no. 1 (January 2005), 90–91.

45. Sang Hyun Lee, "Editor's Introduction," in *Writings on the Trinity, Grace, and Faith,* The Works of Jonathan Edwards, vol. 21, ed. Sang Hyun Lee (New Haven, CT: Yale University Press, 2002), 38–39.

46. Ibid., 40.

47. Jonathan Edwards, "Miscellany 220," in *The Miscellanies*, The Works of Jonathan Edwards, vol. 13, ed. Thomas A. Schafer (New Haven, CT: Yale University Press, 1994).

48. Douglas A. Sweeney, *The American Evangelical Story: A History of the Movement* (Grand Rapids: Baker, 2005), 114–15.

49. Ibid., 68.

50. Timothy Mather Cooley, *Sketches of the Life and Character of the Rev. Lemuel Haynes* (New York: Harper and Brothers, 1837), 91.

51. Richard Allen, *The Life, Experience, and Gospel Labours of the Rt. Rev. Richard Allen*, (Philadelphia: Martin & Boden, 1833), 46.

52. See http://www.africa.upenn.edu/Articles_Gen/Letter_Birmingham.html.

53. R. A. Whitacre, *John,* Vol. 4 (Downers Grove, IL: InterVarsity Press, 1999), 75–76.

54. Ibid., 76.

55. Jerry Bridges, *Transforming Grace: Living Life Confidently in God's Unfailing Love* (Colorado Springs: NavPress, 2008), 196.

56. See http://www.moral-stories.org/the-elephant-chain.

57. Elwell, *Baker Encyclopedia of the Bible*, "Zion."

58. Ibid., "Hell."

59. Chart created and prepared by Docent Research Group upon the request of Eric Mason—a historical summary for key points in Christian history by which grace changed the trajectory of the people of God through a visionary leader promoting grace. See http://www.docentgroup.com.

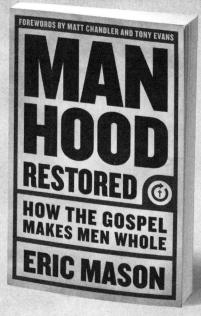

ARE YOU THE MAN GOD INTENDED YOU TO BE?

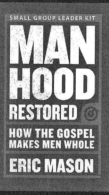

This six-session Bible study combines theological depth with practical insights, putting you and your men's group in step with a gospel-centered manhood that directs you back to God's original intent for your lives.

Dr. Eric Mason is the co-founder and lead pastor of Epiphany Fellowship in Philadelphia and the president of Thriving, a ministry dedicated to aiding ethnic minorities to be resourced and trained for ministry to the urban context.